Union Planters Bank, Memphis, Tennessee

Since Before the Yellow Fever

A History of Union Planters Bank

By John Longwith

Union Planters Corporation
Memphis, Tennessee
1994

Contents

Preface

"There are two reasons why a man does anything," said J. Pierpont Morgan. "There's a good reason, and there's the real reason." In writing this history of Union Planters Bank, I have tried to get at the underlying causes of events, to show some of the "real" reasons why people acted in certain ways and why things turned out as they did. Although this is a commissioned work, my patrons at Union Planters have allowed me a good deal of freedom to look beneath the surface of events and to recount the bank's development as I understand it.

I could not have completed my task without the cooperation of several archivists who helped me flesh out the historical record. Among the staff members of those institutions cited in the Notes and Sources section, I am especially indebted to Barbara LaPointe, Memphis-Shelby County Public Library; Wayne C. Moore and Mary Dessypris, Tennessee State Library and Archives; Bill Short, Burrow Library, Rhodes College; and Richard Schrader, Southern Historical Collection, University of North Carolina at Chapel Hill.

Many people consented to interviews during the course of my research, and I am grateful to those who shared their recollections with me: Vance J. Alexander, Jr., Frank Allen, Robert Barnard, Bess Barry, Jack Beasley, Andrew Benedict, Mildred Blaine, Shirley Bowker, Lucius Burch, Jr., Jack Bulliner, John Burnett III, Loretta Cartwright, Max Cobb, Robert Colbert, Jr., Willis Connell, Jr., James A. Cook, Jr., Giles Coors, Joe Davis, O. K. Earp, Jr., William Ferris, Leo Fristrom, William D. Galbreath, Riley C. Garner, Thomas A. Garrison, Henry Goddard, C. Niles Grosvenor III, Carlton Hays, John Hembree, E. Rex Hogan, William Irvine, Fred Jenkins, Bob Johnson, Denise Kelsoe, George Kinney, Jimmy Lancaster, Lynn Lanigan, Robert Lloyd, and C. J. Lowrance III.

And also: Bob McDonald, Lee McGinnis, Marion Maddox, Robert F. Meurer, Dorsey Newbern, Thomas O'Brien, Edward P. Peacock III, John Pepin, Susan Phillips, J. Walter Pinner, T. J. Pond, Ben Price, Charles Rauscher, Benjamin W. Rawlins, Jr., Brenda Riba, Joe Rives, Mary Elizabeth Rives, Ruth Rossett, Olivia Sauls, Peyton Self III, J. Armistead Smith, James F. Springfield, Leslie M. Stratton III, Edward Thompson, Timmons

Treadwell III, Richard A. Trippeer, Jr., David M. Tucker, James Walker, Claire Watts, Eustace Winn, Jr., Jerry Wood, and Russell Wood.

I also want to thank Dr. John E. Harkins for reading and commenting on the manuscript. John probably has forgotten more about Memphis history than I have learned in my research. His critical reading of the manuscript has preserved me from more than one inaccuracy.

Finally, I am indebted to Ben Rawlins and Jim Springfield, who had faith in this project and showed forebearance when the writing fell behind schedule. Their confidence in the value of this undertaking has been a source of quiet energy for me over these many months of work.

April 1994   J. L.

Since Before
the Yellow Fever

CHAPTER 1

Fortunes of War

*The great profit now made is converting
everybody into rascals.*
—W. T. Sherman to U. S. Grant,
Memphis, October 9, 1862

*I will venture to say that no honest man
has made money in West Tennessee in the
last year, whilst many fortunes have been
made there during that time.*
—Grant to Salmon P. Chase,
July 31, 1863

THE crowd of spectators lining the river bluff in Memphis at sunrise, June 6, 1862, was several thousand strong and still growing. They far outnumbered the officers and crews aboard the eight Confederate gunships that were about to open fire on a flotilla of Federal ironclads steaming slowly toward them in line of battle. Repeated appeals to take up arms and repel these Yankee invaders had left the spectators on the bluff unmoved. What business was it of theirs to oppose the occupation of Memphis? After all, the Confederacy had written the town off as a dead loss. Fire-eaters had become scarce in Memphis, most of the class having migrated south after the fall of New Orleans. Two days ago General P. T. G. Beauregard had ordered his troops out of Memphis, and they had marched off after torching some three hundred thousand bales of cotton, pouring thousands of barrels of molasses down the riverbank, and seizing all the supplies they could carry away. Now the town was garrisoned by a token force under the "Swamp Fox of the Confederacy," General Merriwether Jefferson Thompson. General Thompson cut a dashing figure as he moved among the spectators on the bluff, dressed to kill in sword and sash and red-feathered cockade hat.

On the river below, the artillery duel went on for fifteen minutes with neither side scoring a decisive hit. Then two unarmed and unarmoured rams, built and commanded by the Union engineer of genius Charles Ellet, darted from behind the ironclads and rammed the Confederate gunship *Lovell,* sinking it. The C. S. A. *Beauregard* counter-attacked, only to miss its target and plough into and cripple its own consort ship, the *Price.* Enveloped by blinding smoke, the battered Confederate fleet turned to escape downriver. Only the *Van Dorn* made it to safety. In a little under seventy minutes, the Federal flotilla had captured, burned, or sunk practically the entire Confederate River Defense Fleet, at a cost of one disabled ram and a single casualty (Colonel Ellet, who later died of wounds).

Some firebrands watching from the safety of the bluff vowed never to submit to Yankee rule. Cooler heads, however, were in the majority, particularly among the cotton brokers, the dry goods merchants, and the wholesale grocers. As they saw it, Federal rule could hardly be other than an improvement over the Confederate government, which had imposed martial law, appropriated or destroyed over a hundred million dollars worth of private goods, and finally abandoned the town. These realists included three young businessmen named Farrington, Read, and Hill, who would be remembered in Memphis decades after the name of the Confederate Swamp Fox had faded from memory.

The first of them was William Martin Farrington, a clever, opinionated man with a slightly pinched look about him. Farrington had grown up in the cotton lands around Brownsville, Tennessee, moved to Memphis in 1841 to grade cotton for his brother-in-law, and by 1852 was running his own dry goods and wholesale grocery house of Farrington and Howell. He was also a junior partner in the railroad and land ventures of Memphis' most flamboyant and, some said, wealthiest speculator, Robertson Topp.

In 1838 Topp had bought a 414-acre parcel of densely-wooded land extending south of the town's southern boundary (Union Street) to the river. Over the next decade he cleared and subdivided the land, developing the section along Beale Street into the town's most fashionable address. As the centerpiece of this development, he had built, in 1844, the Gayoso House, whose accommodations were for some years said to rival any to be had in the much older and more cosmopolitan cities of New Orleans and Charleston. It was Topp who had helped Farrington buy into the DeSoto Insurance & Trust Company, a marine and fire insurer formed in 1858 by, among others, Topp's political and business associate, U.S. Senator James C. "Lean Jimmy" Jones. One of the company's specialties was insuring the

steamboats that plied the stretch of the Mississippi from Cairo to New Orleans. With snags, sandbars, and boiler explosions cutting a steamboat's
average length of service to five years, the DeSoto Insurance & Trust could
expect to pay frequent, sizable claims. But the premiums collected were
"sky high," and the chance to insure blockade runners would be especially
lucrative.[1]

The same year that Farrington became president of DeSoto Insurance,
1860, he was elected a director of the local branch of Planters Bank. To be
associated with the second oldest bank in Memphis was no small accom-
plishment for a man who was still two years shy of his fortieth birthday.
But his connection was brief. When the Planters began buying Confederate bonds, Farrington resigned, and he undoubtedly deplored General
Beauregard's decision to commandeer the bank's assets and ship them
south. But the restoration of Federal authority in Memphis promised to
open up new business possibilities for Farrington, if for no other reason
than because Robertson Topp possessed many valuable contacts in Washington and among the Treasury agents who would be regulating the local
commerce in cotton, dry goods, food, and medicine. Farrington and
Topp's relations grew closer during the war years, and in 1867 Topp's
daughter, Florence, became Mrs. William M. Farrington.[2]

Another spectator on the bluff who took a businesslike attitude toward
the Confederate defeat was Samuel P. Read. Like Farrington, Samuel Read
had spent his early years in the West Tennessee town of Brownsville,
clerking in a country store, and then moving to Memphis, in 1857, to manage the cotton and supply business of Edgar McDavitt. Now Read was
within a few weeks of switching from the cotton to the dry goods trade, as
a partner in the firm of Howell, Wood & Read. Cloth and braid and but-
tons for Confederate uniforms would soon command fabulous prices, as
the partners of Howell, Wood & Read correctly surmised. The senior
member of that firm, William H. Wood, happened to be the father-in-law
of another spectator on the bluff who was also busy calculating how to
profit from the new order in Memphis. His name was Napoleon Hill.[3]

Hill was a ruddy-faced bear of a man with twinkling eyes and a sly grin
almost hidden beneath a mustache and beard that were at times bespattered
with tobacco juice. At the age of thirty-two, he was fifteen years away
from owning the largest cotton and supply house in the nation, as well as
a fair chunk of downtown Memphis, controlling interest in three local insurance companies, a street railway, and coal mining lands in Alabama. He
possessed next to no formal education, his father having died in 1844,

leaving the family—of which fourteen-year-old Napoleon was the eldest of nine children—an estate consisting of one heavily-mortgaged plantation in the frontier lowlands of Marshall County, Mississippi. Two years of the pestilential climate and a volatile cotton market were enough. Swallowing their pride, the Hills went to live with relatives in Bolivar, Tennessee, where Napoleon clerked in his uncle's general store. Their dependence on the kindness of kin didn't last long, however. It ended when Napoleon's mother married a well-to-do Memphis gentleman by the name of Josiah DeLoach. This freed Napoleon to seek his own fortune, and in 1849, joining the greatest mass movement of people since the Crusades, he headed for the gold fields of California.

The discovery of gold at Sutter's sawmill near Sacramento had touched off a form of temporary insanity in large segments of the population. Hundreds of ships at anchor in San Francisco Harbor were abandoned; their crews, reportedly, had deserted to search for the mother lode—and so did the soldiers sent to capture them. In time, though, many of these '49ers came to their senses. Some gave up and returned home. Others found steady work for wages. Still others, the smart ones, figured out that the most profitable kind of mining was not being done by the prospectors but by the merchants who were selling potatoes for $1.50 each, an apple for $5.00, an egg for $1.00. Napoleon Hill was one of the smart ones. "Only fools work with their hands," he liked to say. "Smart men work with their heads."[4] And so he opened a combination "drinkerie" and grocery at a spot on the Sacramento convenient to the thirsty miners. Six years later he had his stake: fifteen thousand dollars in gold.[5]

Returning to Bolivar, Hill married Mary Wood, a first cousin of President James K. Polk. On their wedding day in July 1858, a coach drawn by six white horses raced into the Woods's drive. Gripping the reins of three horses in each of his hands, Napoleon Hill pulled to a stop in a cloud of dust. Mrs. Wood took one look at the spectacle and burst into tears. But her husband, not to be upstaged, arranged his own piece of bravado. On a massive silver tray he stacked hundreds of silver coins and had two husky slaves present the gift to Napoleon and Mary. Wood also gave the newlyweds a house at 93 Court Street in Memphis, where Hill had started his cotton and supply business in 1857.

The firm was largely undamaged by the retreating Confederate army, and the imminent arrival of Federal troops posed no apparent danger to it, for Hill had hidden most of its goods and cotton at his farm outside Bolivar.

As the June 6 battle ended, Flag Officer Charles Davis, commander of the Federal flotilla, moved swiftly. He saw no reason to postpone the occupation of Memphis until land forces moving toward the town arrived, as they were scheduled to, within hours. An hour after the battle he dispatched a landing party of three soldiers and a cadet. They made their way to the Post Office building and, surrounded by an unruly but harmless mob, hoisted the National flag. One shot was fired, no one knows by whom.

By that time Confederate General Jeff Thompson was nowhere to be found. One story has it that the "Swamp Fox of the Confederacy" had mounted his horse, announced that he was going "to pay a note in Holly Springs," and galloped away. Napoleon Hill temporarily "retired to his Sabine farm" in West Tennessee. Samuel Read stayed on to enter the dry goods trade. And William Farrington remained to mind his own business, which, he told a friend, "was merchandising and not fighting. I shall try to sell my goods regardless of the flag that floats over us."[7] That would not prove difficult. For several weeks a fleet of trading boats had been following the Federal ironclads like pilot fish. Even before the Stars and Stripes had reached shore, the trading boats were tied up at the landing and doing a brisk trade.[8]

Reporting from Memphis in the spring of 1863, Charles Dana observed:

The mania for sudden fortunes in cotton raging in a vast population of Yankees scattered throughout the country and in this town has to a large extent corrupted and demoralized the army. Every colonel, captain, and quartermaster is in secret partnership with some operator in cotton; while every soldier dreams of adding a bale of cotton to his pay.

Cotton had reached the unheard-of price of one dollar a pound, and President Lincoln, fearing that any move to cut the supply going north would alienate important pro-Union factions in the upper Mississippi Valley, had instructed the army to aid the Treasury Department in speeding the flow of cotton from Southern sellers to Northern buyers.

This vigorous traffic between two regions at war was a sore point for General Ulysses S. Grant, whose own father had decamped in Memphis with a force of three peddlers. "Men who had enlisted to fight the battles of their country," wrote Grant in his *Personal Memoirs,* "did not like to be engaged in protecting a traffic which went to the support of an enemy they had to fight, and the profits of which went to men who shared nothing of the dangers." The policy of trading with the South while making war on it moved Senator Collamer to suggest sardonically that the government "withdraw the army and enlist a large force of Yankee peddlers . . . to go down there and trade them all out; clean them out in trade."

But Lincoln was prepared to accept the evil of profiteering rather than risk the greater evil of break-away border states. In any case, he knew that the trading frenzy was unstoppable; the profit motive was simply too strong. A merchant could sell his cotton for one dollar a pound, buy salt at $1.25 a sack, then turn around and sell the salt anywhere outside Federal lines for $60.00 a sack. Similar profits also awaited him in quinine, lead, flour, bacon, and cloth, all of which brought exorbitant prices behind Southern lines.

Through transactions of this kind a substantial number of Memphians, including Napoleon Hill and William Farrington, emerged from the war financially better off than they had been at the outbreak of hostilities. From his "Sabine farm," Hill had sold cotton for gold, greenbacks, and goods. On top of that, he had acquired access to the new administration in Washington, thanks to his step-father Josiah DeLoach. Back in June 1863 a timely warning from DeLoach had enabled General Grant to elude almost certain capture by Confederate cavalry operating twenty miles east of Memphis. Grant, now in the White House, repaid the favor by appointing his "personal friend," DeLoach, Postmaster of Memphis. From that office DeLoach dispensed Federal patronage locally. As a result, Napoleon Hill could be assured that the Reconstruction policies of the Grant Administration were unlikely to inconvenience him personally.[9]

Moreover, Hill's friends in high places also included the Governor-elect of Mississippi: James Lusk Alcorn. A moderate Republican in a fiercely Democratic state, Alcorn had had no use for Jefferson Davis or the war and, like Hill, had passed the war years selling cotton from his plantation, Eagle's Nest, in Coahoma County, Mississippi.[10]

But Hill was much too shrewd to let himself become closely identified with "scalawags" (native-born whites who supported the Republican Party). Early in 1869 he joined other Memphis businessmen in persuading Jefferson Davis to accept the presidency of the town's Carolina Life Insurance Company. The Hills received calls not only from DeLoach and Alcorn but, according to Mrs. Hill, from "the Semmes [Confederate Rear Admiral Raphael Semmes] and Jefferson Davis."[11]

The war years had been equally kind to William Farrington. His business enjoyed "the most successful period in [its] history during the occupation of Memphis," he was later to say.[12] And he too had come out of the war with business and political connections so diverse as to suggest that the line between scalawags and Southern loyalists was by no means hard and fast. In 1864, by order of the Federal military government, Farrington had taken a seat on the city council. Together with an organizer of Memphis' First National Bank, the Radical Republican head of the Metropolitan Police, S. B. Beaumont, Farrington and others formed the Memphis City Railroad Company, in 1865.[13] On the other hand, Farrington joined Confederate General Gideon Pillow in promoting the Chinese Labor Convention of 1869, an abortive scheme to replace freedmen in the cotton fields with thousands of imported, indentured Chinese.[14] Lending his name to that scheme was Nathan Bedford Forrest, the "Confederacy's wizard of the saddle"—or as Sherman had called him, "that devil." After Forrest went broke in the Panic of 1873, Farrington often visited him in the evenings.[15]

For William Farrington, the war and its immediate aftermath had indeed been a "most profitable period." But that era of windfall profits and easy money was over. The price of cotton had fallen from its peak of $1.44 a pound in mid-1864 to 29 cents in 1868, and to 24 cents in 1869. Almost half a billion dollars in greenbacks issued during the war had been pulled from circulation, and the paper money once issued by state banks had been taxed out of existence by the National Banking Act of 1864. The money supply was rapidly shrinking back to the level of 1860 (by 1884 the national price level was still the same as it had been in 1860). This "Great Deflation," as it came to be known, caught Farrington just as he had invested large sums in the Memphis City Railroad Company and in the Memphis & Little Rock Railroad.[16] Neither of the lines was nearing completion, and both were financially troubled in late 1868. It was then that Farrington decided to organize the bank.

He could not have chosen a business whose prospects looked much dimmer than banking's did in 1868, at least in the South. Five of Memphis' banks had either failed or were about to fail or cease to operate that year. When one of them, the Gayoso Savings Bank, shut its doors, angry depositors stormed the house of its president and forced him to deliver the bank's assets to receivers before permitting him to leave town. Other differences of opinion were sometimes resolved by the revolver or Bowie knife; a long-running feud between directors and creditors of the Farmers and Merchants Bank had been settled by a gunfight in which one group of combatants, their ammunition exhausted, "closed in with knives."[17] Not surprisingly, the life expectancy of banks was none too encouraging, either. Only two banks that had been operating in 1860 were still in existence in 1868.

In another respect, however, Farrington's timing could hardly have been better, for the State of Tennessee was preparing to strike the constitutional provision that allowed the incorporation of tax-exempt banks.[18] With his advance knowledge that a state constitutional convention, scheduled to convene in January 1870, was likely to put a stop to "special incorporations," Farrington had a potent selling point to use in soliciting stock subscriptions. His plan was to convert the DeSoto Insurance Company into a bank, and five of his eight fellow directors at DeSoto approved of his plan. All were familiar names in local business circles: wholesale grocer Charles Wesley (C. W.) Goyer, cotton factor W. B. Galbreath, and steamboat line owner Charles B. Church.

Another director voting with Farrington was J. J. Rawlings, whose commercial career got started in 1824 when his uncle, Ike Rawlings, hired him to translate the Chickasaw spoken by the Indians who traded at Ike's store. Recalling those frontier days, Rawlings wrote, "I knew just enough of the language to have unspeakable fun with the [Chickasaw] girls."[19] Rawlings, secretary and treasurer of Charlie Church's steamboat line, had served on the board of the old Branch Union Bank, whose assets had been commandeered by the Confederate authorities.

The fifth vote for Farrington's proposed conversion was cast by William Borden Greenlaw, the contractor for Robertson Topp's Gayoso House, the developer of a North Memphis subdivision known as the Greenlaw Addition, and owner of the Greenlaw Opera House at Union and Second. In 1861 Greenlaw and his brother had owned the fourth most valuable portfolio of real estate in Memphis. Since then, however, his net worth had become increasingly difficult to calculate. Like Farrington, Greenlaw had invested heavily in the problem-ridden Memphis & Little Rock Railroad.[20]

On February 12, 1869, Farrington secured the passage of a legislative act that enabled DeSoto Insurance to convert to the banking business. All that was required for the switch was the stockholders' approval, and it was obtained on June 1. All marine casualty policies were cancelled forthwith, and the fire risks in force were re-insured through People's Insurance, a firm in which Farrington, Goyer, and Greenlaw were the principals.

Whether Farrington was responsible for naming the new bank is now anybody's guess. But whoever the name-giver was, he knew what he was doing when he called it the Union and Planters Bank of Memphis. On hearing that name, almost anyone in Memphis would have associated the new bank with two Memphis banks of the past: the Branch Union Bank and the Branch Planters Bank. Both had earned the public's confidence during the 1840s and 1850s. Neither could continue after having its assets seized and shipped south in May of 1862, but both eventually returned and distributed to creditors what remained of the assets. The name *Union and Planters* suggested that this new bank would possess the combined strength of its two namesakes.

By the first week of August 1869, Farrington, Greenlaw, and the others had managed to find buyers for $671,300 of Union and Planters stock.[21] That sum was little short of remarkable, considering that it was roughly four times the capitalization of the town's leading bank, the German National. And the list of subscribers included some of the most talented businessmen Memphis had produced. When these stockholders held their first meeting, on August 23, they elected a board of fifteen directors whose expertise ranged from cotton and railroads to steamboats and saloons. Besides the six former directors of DeSoto Insurance—Greenlaw, Goyer, Rawlings, Church, and Farrington—there was Napoleon Hill. His presence gave Union and Planters a one-man clearinghouse of information on the cotton market.

Other cotton factors elected to the board were Nathan Adams of Stanton Depot, James Rogers of Brownsville, and William A. Williamson of Somerville. Williamson, who owned four thousand acres in Hardeman County, was both a planter and a financier; recently he had joined Napoleon Hill and others in organizing the Memphis Gas Light Company. Also elected were cotton factors M. L. Meacham and Zeno Newton Estes.

Another of the directors was the mayor-elect of Memphis, John Johnson. A native of Ireland, Johnson had been orphaned at the age of thirteen, then came to Memphis when he was fourteen, and spent the next four years trading with the Indians along remote stretches of Arkansas' St. Francis River.

Memphis' heterogeneous population was further reflected in the presence of Director Antonio Vaccaro. Born in a village outside Genoa, Italy, Vaccaro had sold cigars on the street corners after landing in Memphis. From street vendor to saloonkeeper, he had worked his way up to ownership of a wholesale wine and liquor company. Rounding out the board was the sole manufacturer in the group: Joseph Bruce, head of Lilly Carriage Company.

In many ways they were a well-matched group. All had started out without benefit of inherited wealth; most had seen their first successes as traders on the fringes of society: Hill in the California gold fields, Rawlings and Johnson trading with the Chickasaw, Goyer with the flatboatmen who by turns had enriched and terrorized Memphis in the 1840s. None had put on either a gray or a blue uniform during the war. Politically they were old-line Whigs who backed the candidates favoring commercial interests: Rawlings would go so far as to assert that the conservative financial policies of the Cleveland Administration made "Grover Cleveland . . . the best President we ever had, Washington not excepted."[22] And in due time Cleveland named Farrington Postmaster of Memphis.[23]

Taken as a group, the directors represented every important line of business in Memphis. Every line, that is, except one. None had experience as a professional, full-time banker. William Williamson, however, had served briefly as president of a country bank; the board elected him vice-president. Farrington, besides being the bank's prime mover, knew his way around the New York banking houses where Union and Planters would maintain correspondent balances; the board elected him the bank's president.

But neither the president nor the vice-president would carry out the day to day duties of chief operating officer. That job belonged to the cashier. His duties covered the essentials: judging credit worthiness and sitting on the discount committee where a note or a bill of exchange was rejected if any one member opposed it. He also signed "all checks" and was responsible for taking "special charge and care of the cash," of which he was to keep "a large proportion under his own lock." He was the gatekeeper, the internal regulator, the man responsible. The position commanded the top salary at the bank ($5,500), higher even than that paid the president ($4,500). For the office of cashier the board elected Farrington's choice, Samuel P. Read, who had left the dry goods trade to become secretary of People's Insurance Company. Although not a banker by training or experience, Read had all the right instincts for the cashier's post. And while a seat on the board did not come with that post, Read's influence on Union and Planters would be as long-lasting as that of any director in the room, with the possible exception of Napoleon Hill.

Before adjourning, the directors agreed to locate the bank in the center of Memphis' financial district, at 11 Madison Street (now 73 Madison Avenue), in a three-story brownstone owned by Director Greenlaw. The purchase price was set at thirty thousand dollars, payable to Greenlaw in Union and Planters stock. Rather than mark time while the building was under construction, they decided to house the bank temporarily in the office of People's Insurance, situated across the street at 16 Madison (now 80 Madison).

News of the bank's formation and its plans to open on September 1, 1869, appeared in the Memphis *Daily Appeal* the day of the board meeting. The *Daily Appeal* paid particular attention to the fact that Union and Planters would increase the town's total banking capital by nearly a third. "This institution will be of the greatest possible benefit to our city," the paper predicted, "and is demanded by the business community. It will afford a monetary relief much needed and we hope will be conducted upon so liberal a scale as to conduce altogether to that end." Just how "liberal a scale" Union and Planters could afford was one matter that the directors had not yet settled.

CHAPTER
2

"A Vast Pawn Shop"

The history of banking in this country is not pleasant for the stockholders to review.

—William M. Farrington, 1874

A CUSTOMER who made the acquaintance of the cashier, the teller, the general bookkeeper, and the individual bookkeeper had met the entire staff of Union and Planters on opening day, Wednesday, September 1, 1869. Although the rash of bank failures had produced a glut of unemployed tellers and bookkeepers willing to work cheaply, Farrington and Read had picked their staff in a way that gave substance to the bank's slogan of "none but the best are needed." James McRae, formerly with the Bank of Tennessee, was employed as individual bookkeeper. The somewhat more responsible position of general bookkeeper went to Louis Czapski, "a fine mathematician," whose loyalty would soon be put to the severest of tests.

Most notable, however, was the choice of teller: James Adolphus Omberg. Irish on one side of his family and Norwegian on the other, Omberg had entered banking at age fifteen as a clerk at the Bank of Chattanooga. When Tennessee left the Union, Omberg had left the post of teller at Memphis' Commercial Bank to fight on the Confederate side. Following Appomattox he had returned to the Commercial only to see it fail. But such was the town's regard for Omberg that he was appointed the bank's receiver, and closed out its affairs to the satisfaction of all. Omberg's talents eventually exceeded his opportunities at Union and Planters; in 1879 he resigned to accept the post of cashier at the Bank of Commerce (reorganized as the National Bank of Commerce in 1933), and in 1907 he was elected president of the First National Bank (re-named First Tennessee Bank in 1977).

Although the bank's own directors constituted its most active loan customers—the first note discounted was Farrington's for $35,000—it could not be fairly said, as Judge Baldwin did of Southern free banks in the 1830s, that Union and Planters "generously loaned all the directors could not use themselves."[1] Rather, the bank offered its services and a decent portion of lendable funds to those having no financial interest in the bank. Jefferson Davis opened a checking account. James Lusk Alcorn and Gideon Pillow borrowed from Union and Planters, as did Pillow's law partner, ex-Governor Isham G. Harris, whose life had become more settled since the time when the Radical Republicans' reward of five thousand dollars for his capture had forced him to flee the country. Other borrowers included German-born merchant Elias Lowenstein, the A. Schwab Company, and Robert Bogardus Snowden, a New Yorker who had moved south, fought under the stars-and-bars at Chickamauga, and then married the granddaughter of John Overton, the land speculator responsible together with Andrew Jackson and James Winchester for founding Memphis in 1819.[2]

While Cashier Read minded the bank's daily transactions, President Farrington passed much of his time in New York, arranging correspondent accounts or, during the winter of 1869–70, huddling with state legislators in Nashville. Despite an argumentative nature that embroiled him in at least one, often two or more law suits every year for the next two decades, Farrington could be a master of persuasion in the right circumstances. In the backrooms of the state capitol, "cooperating with others," Farrington "set on foot efforts" that resulted in a legislative act raising the maximum legal rate of interest from six percent to ten percent.

Even more valuable to Union and Planters was the other prize Farrington brought back from Nashville. The First National of Memphis had been the West Tennessee bank of deposit for state funds during the Radical Republican governorship of William G. "Parson" Brownlow. After Brownlow vacated the governor's mansion for the U.S. Senate, state money had stayed at First National, till February 1870, when Farrington succeeded in having Union and Planters designated as the state's depository in West

Tennessee. The account was by far the bank's single largest, sometimes carrying a balance approaching one million dollars.[3]

By April 1870 profits and prospects looked good enough for the board to declare a six percent dividend, payable semiannually. Total notes and discounts stood at $339,648, there was cash on hand of $218,229, and during the first half of the year net earnings amounted to a respectable $30,000.

If the directors had any reason to feel a bit uneasy, that feeling had to do with the region's chronically troubled economy. True, Memphis boasted twice the population of Atlanta, and the influx of twelve thousand newcomers since 1865 had swelled its population to 39,400, which was but a few thousand short of Charleston's population. Granted, too, the town's business people had many reasons to suppose that, as one historian phrased it, "no Southern town was more likely to become the first depot of northern capitalists than Memphis." But there were two serious, if still latent, problems with this view of Memphis as the future "Chicago of the lower West."[4]

Memphis' prime source of income, the basis of its credit, and the foundation of its banking system all depended on each year's highly speculative cotton crop, the value of which had steadily declined, from twenty-nine cents a pound in 1868 to seventeen cents in 1870. Not only was the market headed downward, but the cotton-growing Delta was little better off than it had been five years before. With the loss of every third horse and mule and the destruction of almost half the region's farm machinery, productive capacity had dropped. Thousands of freedmen lived from hand to mouth in a free labor market without the cash to pay them wages. State treasuries were dangerously depleted: in 1866, Mississippi had spent one-fifth of its entire revenues on artificial arms and legs. Moreover, the Mississippi and Arkansas Delta badly needed levees to stop the river from periodically overflowing into the rich bottomlands.

But obtaining Federal money for Southern public works projects was about as easy as squeezing water from a cotton bale; of the $103 million appropriated by Congress for internal improvements between 1865 and 1873, New York and Massachusetts alone received $21 million, while Arkansas and Mississippi got $185,000.

Cotton cropping seemed a risky proposition to many planters, including the one who wrote Napoleon Hill with this offer: "I propose to rent my plantation 1300 acres in a high state of cultivation 45 Negroes on the place that never left. . . . Make any reasonable arrangement with any party that will take the place."[5] As more and more plantations like this one were worked by tenants and sharecroppers, the region's productive capacity became organized along lines strikingly similar to those of Europe in medieval times.

While tenants and sharecroppers worked the fields much as serfs had done in feudal Europe, the planter's resemblance to a lord of the manor usually ended when he sought financing. His land was all but valueless as collateral, and abolition had destroyed the very basis of credit. In place of loans secured by the human collateral of slaves, there had evolved "one of the strangest contractual relationships in the history of finance": namely, the crop-lien system. By its terms a planter who required seed money went to his cotton factor and pledged his unplanted crop to secure a loan at eight to twelve percent interest. But the planter's total cost—and the factor's total profit—were considerably more than eight to ten percent. Even though only a set percentage of the loan could be drawn each month, the rate charged was as if the planter had use of the total sum from the start.

The planter also paid the factor or furnishing merchant a "credit price" that could be fifty percent higher than the cash price charged for the supplies he needed to see him through till harvest. After the cotton was harvested and sold he then paid his factor a commission fee of 2 1/2 to 4 percent. Add a few more percent in fees for fire insurance and warehousing, paid to factors like Napoleon Hill who owned such businesses, and the planter's total indebtedness could rise to twice the principal sum of the loan.

Once bound to a factor, the planter was seldom able to look for better terms elsewhere, because the factor held a mortgage on the planter's land, not just for one growing season but for a fixed term of years. The crop-lien system of financing had the effect, observed C. Vann Woodward, of "convert[ing] the Southern economy into a vast pawn shop."

The other threat to Memphis' future was a municipal government in which corruption, incompetence, and greed had combined to produce a staggering public debt, with nothing much to show for it. Perhaps the best-known example of municipal waste was the Nicholson pavement project. In 1867 a million dollars had disappeared into paving the business district with small pine blocks mortised with pitch and cement; by 1870 those pitch-and-pine-paved streets, already in an alarming state of decay, were absorbing slops and garbage, which fertilized the melon plants growing from cracks in the streets.

This and similar expenditures had pushed municipal indebtedness to

nearly four million dollars, on which interest coupons rarely were re-
deemed at maturity. New York banks had shut off the town's credit in
1868. Tax collections were starting to fall, and in a self-defeating attempt
to stave off civic insolvency the aldermen were issuing scrip that was
negotiable at only sixty-five percent of face value, but redeemable at
par.

Worse, nobody appeared able or willing to sound the depths of this
ocean of debt. "Committees were lost in its intricacies and inaccuracies,"
reports an eyewitness, J. M. Keating, editor of the *Commercial Appeal*.
"The comptroller managed at the end of the year [1869] to make a report
in which the debit almost balanced the credit side, inducing the belief that
Memphis had assets to meet her liabilities, assets that became more and
more shadowy, and gradually disappeared the nearer the hand of settlement reached out for them."

Such was the financial shop of horrors that Union and Planters' Director John Johnson stepped into as Memphis' new mayor. When Johnson
took office in January 1870, he found

> the city without a dollar of cash in her treasury, and her credit so im-
> paired that she was really paying at least two prices for all services
> rendered, or supplies purchased; her bonds, authorized to be issued to
> fund due outstanding indebtedness, having been and being disposed
> of by her own officers at less than fifty cents on the dollar; and though
> ostensibly the pay of city employees and [the cost of] supplies ob-
> tained were at cash rates, yet by allowances thereon in various ways,
> and for heavy interest on loans, and fabulous discounts on bonds sold,
> the cost to the city was eventually more than double the amount nom-
> inally paid.

Attempting to get Memphis out of hock, Mayor Johnson pruned expenses, created a sinking fund, and used the grit of an old Indian trader to
collect back taxes. His "pay-as-you-go" policies reduced municipal debt
by some six hundred thousand dollars, but further austerity measures ran
up against a wall of ward politicians who resented having their snouts
yanked out of the public trough, and citizens who agreed in theory with
Johnson but in practice declined to pay their tax assessments. Before long,
municipal spending would lurch completely out of control.

As both Memphis and the Delta sank deeper in debt, Union and Planters
showed signs of mild distress. Although subscribers to the bank's stock

had paid sixty percent down and agreed to pay the balance in four months, when January 1870 rolled around some of them were short of cash. After another month passed and they were still short, the board instructed the officers to "call upon delinquent stock subscribers and request them to pay up or expunge their names from the subscription book." Cotton planter James Rogers left the board shortly thereafter, to be replaced by cotton factor William A. Goodwyn.

That same year, in December, the directors whittled the dividend down to five percent. A month later the cash on hand was down to $145,040, and discounts up to $456,781, though of that sum only $1,000 was classified past due. On October 25, the board voted to disinvest in municipal Memphis by selling "all Memphis City bonds . . . within thirty days." And like a great many of their counterparts they refused to pay the taxes assessed by the city, the county, and the state. Possibly that refusal had something to do with Mayor Johnson's decision to sell his stock and resign from the board in 1872. Zeno Estes resigned as well, to be replaced by Allison C. "A. C." Treadwell, a rail-thin cotton factor who weighed only 120 pounds but stood six feet two inches tall. Director Goodwyn also chose that time to depart. His seat went to a crusty lawyer named Enoch Ensley, who was described by a biographer as "rugged . . . somewhat dogmatic in asserting [his convictions] . . . disdain[ful] of rules and ornaments . . . admir[ing] an iron furnace or a rollingmill more than he does a landscape or a painting."

Another plausible explanation for the departure of Johnson, Estes, and Goodwyn involves the surprise they received at the board meeting of January 17, 1872. During it the officers reported the astounding fact that overdrafts totalled $263,009. Never before had the topic of overdrawn accounts been mentioned in the official record of the board. Now, suddenly, the directors were given to understand that the bank possessed more overdrafts than it did cash on hand.

When the list of overdrawn customers was read out, the names were unlikely to have come as a relief to the board. Heading the list was the City of Memphis; though only three months ago the board had voted to clear the portfolio of all Memphis bonds, for some reason the officers had proceeded to pay municipal checks drawn on insufficient funds to the tune of $109,572. Merchants who kept "running accounts" were overdrawn by $59,797. The balance of the overdrafts, $93,639, belonged to one of the bank's own directors, William Greenlaw. President Farrington assured the board that the collaterals securing these overdrafts were "ample." Ample or not, the board thought the overdrafts rather "large to remain as they are."[6]

During the summer of 1872 a few directors—Napoleon Hill and C. W. Goyer among them—were beginning to see in the spring avalanche of overdrafts one small piece of a larger problem at Union and Planters. Their suspicions focused on President Farrington. They knew that Farrington, on his own and jointly with Director Greenlaw, had borrowed well over one hundred thousand dollars of the bank's funds. On more than one occasion they had asked Farrington to pay down those loan balances; nevertheless, they had voted to renew the loans at Farrington's urgent request. As a practical matter, Farrington was in no position to reduce his loan balances without liquidating assets in a declining market, and Greenlaw had few liquid assets just then. His fortune of some one million dollars was tied up in the Memphis & Little Rock Railroad, whose treasury needed liberal infusions of capital if the line was ever to be extended beyond the Arkansas swamps where it was stuck. Greenlaw, desperate for funds, had offered to pay the editors of the *Commercial Appeal* a stipend for each editorial they wrote in favor of what amounted to state subsidization of the line.[7]

The financial strain was getting to Greenlaw. Lately he had started administering public tongue-lashings to those who owed him money, including Robertson Topp. As Topp's wife, Elizabeth, later wrote, though "Greenlaw had been indebted to Mr. T for many a lift, as he was climbing the ladder of life and especially for saving his home from being demolished by the federals . . . he made the loan [of $600] the cause of intolerable mortification for Mr. T, dunning him in loud language, even across the street."[8]

While nothing in the bylaws prohibited the president or a director from borrowing every penny of the bank's capital, and though neither Farrington nor Greenlaw apparently intended the bank any harm, Farrington had impaired his credibility as a banker and placed himself in an ethically dubious position by requesting indulgences he would have denied others. Even though his collateral may have been "ample" at the time, he knew as well as Hill and Goyer did how quickly values could fall in a sharp economic downturn. Farrington continued to have his way with the board, but at the price of losing the good will of Hill, Goyer, and a few other directors. For the time being, however, they kept their doubts to themselves.[9]

Memphians who believed in omens had a lot to ponder beginning early in the winter of 1872. The first in a long series of calamities struck in December when an epizoic infection paralyzed the horse-drawn transportation system. Two days after Christmas the river froze, curtailing river traffic and breaking up several million dollars worth of coal barges and steamboats. Food and coal supplies ran low; panicky townspeople stole fence posts to use as firewood, and some of the down-and-out froze or starved to death. Smallpox visited the town later in the winter of 1873, and cholera followed in the spring. By the summer of 1873 the editors of the *Commercial Appeal* were writing that Memphis had seen enough trouble "to last us for a generation. . . . We want to be let alone. We want to make money; we want the prosperity that comes of strict attention to business, and we don't want any more scares or excitements." Their wish did not come true.

The steamtug *Bee,* out of New Orleans, stopped in Memphis one August day just long enough to drop off two passengers who complained of headaches, a raging thirst, pains in the back and legs, and chills alternating with intense sweating. Their stay was brief: soon their skin turned yellow, they began to vomit black blood, and a few hours later they were dead. Their deaths attracted scant notice, surprisingly little notice considering that they had displayed all the classic symptoms of yellow fever, and that the yellow jack was the one health hazard Memphians feared most. What the bubonic plague had been to medieval Europe, yellow fever was to Memphis and the Delta.

But the female *Aëdes aegypti,* a silvery, comparatively noiseless household mosquito, has a tricky way of spreading the virus. After biting an infected victim, the mosquito goes through an incubation period during which the virus remains dormant, harmless. The incubation phase lasts eight to twelve days, sufficient time for observers to conclude that the danger is past. At that point the *Aëdes* can pass the virus on to as many humans as it can bite, and toward the end of August 1873, the "very sociable and man-loving" *Aëdes* was particularly active in Memphis.

On Wednesday, September 17, the Board of Health, after initially having attributed the rising death toll to "congestion," announced that yellow fever was epidemic. More than half the town's white population fled or prepared to escape as the fever spread in all directions from the shantytown area known as Happy Hollow. Those who remained to face the disaster were admired for their courage and compassion. Among them were John Johnson, C. W. Goyer, and also Annie Cook, madam of the Mansion House at 359 Main, who converted her fashionable bordello into a hospital and personally nursed the afflicted. The city aldermen, on the other hand, fled in such numbers that a quorum could not be had to transact the town's business. Napoleon Hill headed for St. Louis and William Farrington set off for Kentucky, but Samuel Read, his staff, and at least four of the bank's directors stayed put. Their worries soon included more than yellow fever.

On Thursday, September 18, word spread throughout the nation that the respected New York banking house of Jay Cooke & Company had suspended because it could no longer meet its obligations. News of the failure touched off a financial panic nationwide. Public faith in banks, never strong even in the best of times, fell to a new low. The rush to close out deposit accounts was on.

Three days after Jay Cooke & Company went under, an "angry and excited mob" of 1,500 Memphians crowded Madison Street, demanding to withdraw their deposits from the town's banks. By closing time at three o'-clock that afternoon, Memphis' seven banks had paid out roughly one million dollars to depositors. The First National Bank, its resources almost exhausted, thereupon "closed for a few days," thus increasing the pressure on the remaining banks.[10]

Conditions at Union and Planters were equally perilous. On September 25, Samuel Read called a special meeting of what remained of the board: C. W. Goyer, William Greenlaw, Enoch Ensley, and A. C. Treadwell. Read had called them together, he explained, because "in view of the fact that the First National had suspended and the possibility of suspension of other banks in the city and a terrible panic now prevailing here and elsewhere," he thought it "prudent" to let the board decide whether or not to keep the bank open.

As matters stood, deposits had been reduced by half during the run, which had tapered off. Slightly more than fifty thousand dollars of the bank's cash was out of reach, locked away in the vaults of its New York correspondent, P. W. Myers Company, which had suspended on September 21. Although President Farrington had gone to New York with the idea of somehow laying hands on the fifty thousand dollars, Read did not think that likely. It was still too early in the season to expect any return on the loans to cotton factors. Furthermore, the yellow fever, which was now striking one out of every three Memphians, might incapacitate the bank's staff at a critical moment.

All in all the picture Read painted was grim. Still, Enoch Ensley and William Greenlaw offered to provide emergency cash out of their own pockets. C. W. Goyer and A. C. Treadwell were still on hand to lend support, as well. And so, "after reviewing the situation" the directors "unanimously resolved that its condition was such as justified . . . that the bank continue to pay currency to all to whom it was due."

That settled, the board adjourned, not to meet again until November 19, 1873—at least not for the record. Unofficially, however, a number of the directors met often to decide what was to be done about President Farrington.

CHAPTER 3

The Bills Fall Due

*Beautiful credit! . . . 'I wasn't worth a
cent two years ago, and now I owe two
millions of dollars.'*
—Twain and Warner, *The Gilded Age*

*Debtors must sometimes be taught there
is earnestness and not play in business
transactions.*
—Union and Planters' Directors Hill, Goyer,
Galbreath, Williamson, Bruce, Treadwell, and
Vaccaro (1874)

FROST came finally late in October 1873 to rid Memphis of the "sociable, man-loving" *Aëdes aegypti.* A week later the yellow fever had run its course: one-third of the fifteen thousand who never left town had sickened, and two thousand died. Samuel Read and his staff of five had kept Union and Planters open all the while and lived to tell about it. Their extreme fidelity earned a resolution of thanks from the board and, "in order to compensate them for extra expenses," the board presented a bonus of two hundred dollars apiece to teller James Omberg, bookkeepers Louis Czapski and W. R. Stewart, and collecting clerks Thomas Darden and John A. Jones. The bonus worked out to roughly one month's salary for each of the men.

Even as the menace of yellow fever receded, economic woes multiplied. Summing up local conditions in 1874, the Chamber of Commerce reported: "Everywhere there has been stagnation, money lying unemployed, labor languishing for want of work, machinery idle, railroads left unfinished, and many a grand scheme suspended, that under happier auspices would have created incalculable wealth."

Bedford Forrest's plan to build a railroad from Holly Springs to the iron and coal lands of Alabama had foundered, bankrupting him in the process. Not able to keep up the mortgage on the house he had bought from William Farrington, the "wizard of the saddle" was moving to President's Island, there to farm with convict labor that he leased from the city at ten cents a day.[1] Another victim of hard times was Jefferson Davis. His last fifteen thousand dollars had disappeared when the Carolina Life Insurance Company folded in the Panic of September 1873. Since then the former president of a nation had left his wife, Varina, in Memphis while he wandered rootless again.

Robertson Topp also was ruined financially, his real estate holdings being seized one by one for the back taxes he owed. Topp, gambling on the support of friends close to Lincoln, Andrew Johnson, and Grant, had bought, on the cheap, titles to some one million dollars in cotton impounded by the federal government. But the government refused to acknowledge his cotton claims, and his friends couldn't or wouldn't intervene. Like a character out of *Bleak House,* Topp had become a perpetual plaintiff. He "passed winter after winter in Washington City bringing [his cotton claims] before the Congress and before the Courts." In 1876 he died without having collected anything, and though his son-in-law, William Farrington, pressed the family's claims for decades, nothing except partial payment was received, and that not until 1916, five years after Farrington's death.[2]

Farrington's own situation was precarious, more precarious than he seems to have realized or admitted. The time-sanctioned practice of making money off the capital of others was his specialty, but at Union and Planters he had lost the ability to distinguish between the bank's capital and his own. That, at least, was the conclusion reached by seven of the directors, who happened to know as much, if not more, than Farrington did about trading on the capital of others. They chose to teach him a lesson on leverage when the board convened to elect officers on January 14, 1874.

The "plot," as Farrington liked to call it, was devised and carried out by Directors Hill, Goyer, Galbreath, Treadwell, Bruce, and Vaccaro; Vice-president Williamson joined them shortly before the meeting. What spurred them to act was Farrington's indebtedness. Individually and jointly with Director Greenlaw, he now owed Union and Planters $203,991.97—a sum equal to one-third of the bank's available capital or, in Goyer's words, "sufficient to make a very respectable banking capital." Worse, the Farrington-Greenlaw notes and overdrafts "had been carried by the bank through seasons of peril, when the very existence of the bank might have been endangered thereby. . . [and] continued for years by renewed re-newals, and renewals renewed."

To the dissenting directors there was no longer any doubt that such con-duct demonstrated Farrington's intent "to control the bank in the interest of himself and a friend [Greenlaw] intimately associated with him in finan-cial questions."[3]

Hill, Goyer, and the others knew that Farrington was apt to turn any dif-ference of opinion into a legal or corporate battle royal, that he held a con-siderable number of proxies, and that he could depend on the backing of Directors Ensley, Greenlaw, Church, and Rawlings. Consequently they waited till the last possible moment to strike.

Farrington, blithely ignorant of their intention, voted his proxies to re-elect Hill and the others. Then, minutes before the board was to elect a slate of officers, the salary committee, composed of W. B. Galbreath, A. C. Treadwell, and William Williamson, proposed a drastic change in execu-tive salaries; they moved to raise the cashier from $6,000 to $7,500, and to lower the president from $6,000 to $2,000. When their motion passed by a vote of seven to four, Farrington barely had time to collect his wits before Antonio Vaccaro moved to proceed with the election of president. C. W. Goyer seconded the motion, and on the first ballot Goyer received six votes to Farrington's three.[4] Farrington was out of office almost before he saw the axe falling.

Stunned by the defeat, Farrington persisted in thinking that the board would return him to office once he paid his debts. Psychologically, he ap-peared incapable of accepting the reality of his situation. It was as though he'd had his arm severed at the shoulder but had convinced himself that it was no more than a trifling flesh wound. Nor could he quite grasp that the motive behind the dunning notices from the bank was deadly serious. Only when the bank confiscated and sold his collaterals did he wake up. Embit-tered beyond all reason, he immediately penned, published, and circulated a twenty-three-page broadside, which could not have been much more damaging to his own case if it had been written by his worst enemy. Evi-dently dashed off in a white-hot rage, this "Address to the Stockholders of Union and Planters Bank of Memphis" reveals more about its author than he probably would have cared to show had he been in a calmer state of mind.

In it Farrington portrays himself as the bank's prime mover, an upright financier "badly treated . . . injured [by the] premeditated malice . . . [of directors] who by *my votes* had been placed in a position to thus *strike* at my character."[5] For the most part the key never modulates from the register of high-pitched indignation, in which there sounds the theme of how-could-you-do-this-to-me? interspersed with self-congratulation and melodramatic phrasings such as "the combination against me," "the plot," "mystic crewe," and "my overthrow." President Goyer and Cashier Read are cast as Cassius and Brutus respectively. Read—"the best of friends [whom] I was instrumental in placing . . . in a good position"—stands accused of truckling to the board out of craven self-interest.

However that may have been, the man whose business had taken him safely outside the yellow fever zone was not in the best position to question the loyalty of the man who had so recently risked his life for Union and Planters. (Ironically, Farrington and Read are buried almost side-by-side in Memphis' Elmwood Cemetery.)

It was President Goyer, however, who provoked language strong enough to activate the *code duello.* More than a few "personal meetings"—the local euphemism for duels—had resulted from milder verbal exchanges than the one Farrington tells of having with President Goyer. Following the sale of his collaterals, writes Farrington, he confronted Goyer and "expressed my indignation in a manner that I considered authorized, for I felt that contempt we always feel for one who has not the manliness and independence to rise superior to evil influences, and bad councils."

Farrington undoubtedly was blind to the comic absurdity of questioning the "manliness" of a former flatboatman who had lost his wife to yellow fever in 1867 yet had remained in Memphis to lend a hand during the last epidemic. The absurdity of Farrington's charge would not, however, have been lost on his readers.

Ultimately, though, Farrington undercuts his own arguments and entangles himself in contradictions. In one paragraph he argues that "those chosen [as directors] owe their election to me." Later on he admits that his indebtedness "may appear too large, and, perhaps, it may be so, but it seems that the board either did not so regard it, or were wanting in frankness and independence to express their opinion." Wanting to have it both ways, he first claims to have elected and controlled the board, then he argues that the board ought to have had the backbone to deny him the loans he urgently requested.

Another, more telling, contradiction pops up in the final paragraphs, where he writes: "But, I have drawn from this experience a lesson that, I trust, will be of service both to the bank and myself, and it is this: I am satisfied *no officer,* under any circumstances, *should be permitted to borrow a dollar* from the bank with which he is connected." That, however, was a lesson that Farrington never consistently applied in his own case. While serving as vice-president at the Continental National Bank in 1893, he borrowed from the Continental, fell behind in repayment, and was sacked by the board. In a judgment eerily like the one Goyer had passed on Farrington, C. F. M. Niles, president of the Continental, was to say: "I felt that [Farrington] was not a proper person to be vice president of the bank. . . . I felt that he was inclined to take advantage of his position."[6]

The board's printed response to Farrington's broadside was brief, consistent, and devastating. Signed by President Goyer, Vice-president Williamson, and Directors Hill, Galbreath, Treadwell, Vaccaro, and Bruce, the reply noted that Farrington "has, himself, set forth in his pamphlet . . . of imaginary greivances . . . every argument and fact requisite to convince the stockholders of the imperative necessity [for his removal]."[7] Twice the writer shows a wit that one could sharpen one's fangs on. Of Farrington's whereabouts during the yellow fever epidemic, the author observes: "He was absent, and as prudence is the better part of valor, no doubt he showed good sense in remaining away, thinking it better to live in Kentucky than to die in Tennessee." And on the professions of selfless devotion to the bank, the writer comments: "Mr. Farrington . . . says: 'I congratulate you, as well as myself, that I have never lost sight of your interest.' Possibly there was a typographical error and it should have read 'my interest.' "

While applauding Farrington's belated discovery that no officer ought to borrow from a bank he serves, the directors go on to suggest that Farrington had yet to see the central lesson of the affair. That lesson, says the writer, is: "Debtors must sometimes be taught there is earnestness and not play in business transactions."

With a face that looked like it had been carved from marble, and a beard long and thick enough to warm his chest in winter, President Charles Wesley Goyer resembled a no-nonsense Presbyterian elder, which was what he was. From the violent world of the flatboatmen, Goyer had risen by degrees to become sole proprietor of C. W. Goyer & Company, the largest wholesale grocery house in a town where large wholesale grocery houses were commonplace.

By the 1890s Goyer & Company would take in over a million and a half dollars yearly, own smokehouses capable of holding six hundred thousand pounds of meat at a time, and open branches in eight states, including

Louisiana and Illinois. Nobody doubted that C. W. Goyer was "shrewd"—
the word repeatedly used to describe his predecessor at Union and
Planters, William Farrington. But the word that appears and reappears in
the various accounts of Goyer's life is the word "honorable."

A shrewd and tough president whose honor was widely deemed unim-
peachable was precisely what Union and Planters could not have done
without for the next five years. The good will built up during the epidemic
and Panic was partially dissipated by the public row Farrington had kicked
up. And his management, as well as his ouster, had created a host of internal problems, with potentially disastrous consequences if the economy
continued its downward slide. Most obvious was the high percentage of
doubtful assets. Out of $708,406 in discounts and notes, $111,000 was past
due and another $74,753 was tied up in customer overdrafts, reported the
examining committee on January 21, 1874.

"The bank we do not consider in as good condition oweing to the heavy
loans made to a few parties," the committee members said. Headed by
A. C. Treadwell, the examiners told the board:

> We urgently recommend the heavy loans be reduced as rapidly as
> possible, that the business community may be afforded all facilities,
> thereby building up business for the bank and for the further purpose
> of withstanding future emergencies we would recommend also that
> no discounts in the future be permitted to any officer of this bank un-
> til the same has been ratified by the board at a regular meeting, and
> further that no loans, in excess of $50,000 shall be made to any firm
> or any individual until submitted to and allowed by the board.

The directors duly approved these measures to tighten up credit standards. After five years in business, they were now beginning to decide just
how liberal a scale they meant to operate on.

The meeting produced one other unpleasant but not unexpected item for
the directors to ponder. W. B. Greenlaw announced that he could not pay
back his notes, for "his collateral had been exhausted and . . . he could offer no additional collateral." The board, perhaps appreciating Greenlaw's
frankness, gave him till June to pay up. By then, however, his affairs had
gone from bad to hopeless, and the board voted to "take the usual course"
of seizing his collateral, the value of which had dropped so far that the
board put off their auction.

The directors also had to contend with William Farrington, who held on to his stock for another two years. In the meantime he voted against nearly every measure the others favored, he read lengthy protests into the minutes, he demanded reams of information on the bank's operations, he refused to pay his full share of the debt he had contracted together with Greenlaw, and he filed suit against the bank when it took legal measures to collect.

Although his shrill nit-picking eventually alienated his former allies on the board, his attacks on Read were causing differences among the directors. The differences surfaced at the meeting of January 11, 1875. A new director, Edmond Minetry Apperson, took issue with the salary committee's plan to cut Read's salary almost in half, to four thousand dollars a year. Apperson, like several other men in the board room, was known to face facts head on and speak his mind. In the 1830s he had gone broke on a Mississippi plantation, but had recovered to become owner of the huge Front Street wholesale grocery house that bore his name. He was president of the People's Protective Union, a radically conservative organization whose aim was no less than to turn out the "damn theives" in city hall by repealing Memphis' corporate charter. Moreover, it was Apperson who had acted as executor of the Wade Bolton will, over which seven people had died in a murderous family feud.

Apperson let it be known that he thought the proposed salary of four thousand dollars was too little for Read. He moved to make it six thousand dollars, but the vote wound up tied, and the chairman voted against the measure. At which point Vice-president Williamson proposed to fix Read's salary at $7,500, and the board agreed to it.

What to pay Read became less of an issue later in the year, when Farrington lost his seat on the board, two of his allies died, and a third resigned. W. B. Greenlaw died that summer, as did C. B. Church, and J. J. Rawlings had left to accept the thankless office of county tax assessor. Those four losses, in addition to the two earlier vacancies created by the resignations of M. L. Meacham and Nathan Adams, had brought six new directors to the bank: E. M. Apperson; H. B. Howell, cotton factor and one-time partner of Farrington; dry goods merchant J. F. Frank; cotton factor A. N. McKay, and lawyer M. P. Jarnigan.

As in the past, the directors were the largest borrowers from Union and Planters. Between May 1875 and June of the following year, C. W. Goyer & Company received loans of $220,000, or eleven percent of the bank's total loan volume for the period. The Hill, Fontaine Company borrowed $140,475, the W. B. Galbreath Company $91,431, the A. Vaccaro Company $91,431, and smaller amounts went to Directors McKay, Ensley, Frank, Williamson, Howell, and Treadwell. All together, the directors received thirty-nine percent of the total funds on loan between May 1875 and June 1876.[8]

Placing so large a proportion of funds with directors was not only advantageous to them but also to the bank. With businesses defaulting right and left, it made sense to have funds in strong firms like Hill, Fontaine and the Goyer Company. And nowhere else could Hill, Goyer, or the others obtain funds at lower rates, for interest rates in the South were on their way up to an incredible twenty-four percent.

In the fall of 1875, as the cotton harvest put peak demands on banks and sent waves of illiquidity rippling through the banking system from Wall Street to Madison Street, Samuel Read had to travel as far as Cincinnati to obtain funds—at eighteen percent interest, which at the time was considered a bargain.

On Front Street, marshalls waving writs of mandamus were collecting from the tills of merchants the municipal debts owed by the City of Memphis. In all but name the city was bankrupt; Hill and Apperson, through the People's Protective Union, were calling more forcefully for revocation of the city charter and repudiation of the municipal debt, much of which, they said, was held by "remorseless Shylocks who speculate in city bonds at 21 cents [and] demand their payment dollar for dollar."

Bracing for the "future emergencies" that now looked inevitable, the board reduced capital stock to $600,000 in January 1876. With that, Union and Planters stock would be more salable, more acceptable as collateral—and less of a potential liability to stockholders. In July the examination committee detected "improvement" compared to the year before, but the board suspended the five percent dividend, primarily because assets still included seventy thousand dollars of the unpaid Farrington-Greenlaw notes. Despite all, however, the officers were managing to show a decent profit: $33,436 for the previous six months.

To maintain that level of return the officers pared expenses and, increasingly, looked to money markets beyond the South. Expenditures, which had amounted to some $2,000 monthly in 1874, dropped to about $1,600 a month in 1877. That year Read purchased for the bank two hundred thousand dollars in foreign bonds through the Bank of New York. The next April he went at the board's behest to New York "to lend at the best rate obtainable from two to four hundred thousand dollars upon United States bonds."

As the economic pressure mounted, Read took an unusual initiative. In a letter to the board, dated July 3, 1878, he wrote: "In January 1875 I voluntarily suggested that the Cashier be reduced $1,000. And now in view of the depression in trade and the general stagnation in business I will make a further reduction of $500 and consider my salary at the rate of $6,000 per annum. Hoping you will accept the above in the spirit that it is intended I remain, respectfully [signed] S. P. Read."

Anyone on the board who still had lingering doubts about Read's value would discover within a month that Read's six thousand dollar salary didn't begin to reflect his true worth.

News of yellow fever raging in the West Indies reached Memphis on June 3, 1878. That was unexpectedly early for the onset of a sickly season, but the Board of Health wired New Orleans and Mobile to learn whether any cases of the disease had occurred there. The replies came back negative. By July, however, there were unofficial reports of yellow fever in New Orleans, and on the 30th the first terrified refugees from Grenada, Mississippi, eighty miles to the south, began to stream in with reports that the killer disease had visited Grenada. The Board of Health immediately clamped a quarantine on all passengers arriving from points south. By then it was already too late.

Kate Bionda, a snack shop operator in under-the-hill Happy Hollow, was the first officially acknowledged victim. She died on August 13. Ten days later, when the Board of Health declared an epidemic, the *Appeal* told Memphis: "Let all who can [,] go quickly [,] so that there will be as little food as possible for the pestilence to feed on."

Never before or since has Memphis seen panic such as then broke out. Men knocked down women and children to board trains so overcrowded that passengers were hanging out the windows. Those without tickets boarded with pistols drawn. Thirty thousand fled, leaving a population of twelve thousand blacks and only some six thousand whites. Then the terror began.

"The stench of Memphis sickened me before I got within five miles of the city," wrote Dr. William Ramsey in September. "No words can describe [this] . . . city of horrors . . . the filth I saw, the rotten wooden pavements, the dead animals, putrefying human bodies and the half-buried dead combining to make the atmosphere something fearful."

After the death toll rose to more than one hundred a day, carpenters doubled the price of coffins but still could not meet the demand. Pans of sulphur burned in the halls of the Peabody Hotel, and outside a priest saw "coffins . . . piled up along the street." Looters broke into abandoned stores and offices.

Union and Planters was opened two hours each business day by Samuel Read, his staff, and C. W. Goyer. Read tells of standing outside the bank and looking up and down Madison Street and seeing no signs of human activity, except the occasional rumble of a dead cart or the undertaker's cry of "Bring out your dead." Sometime in September the bank's cashier, the "fine mathematician" Louis Czapski, came down with the disease and died. Read himself was stricken but recovered. His six-year-old daughter, Susan, was not so lucky. She is buried beside him in Elmwood Cemetery.

"This city is almost depopulated," wrote a policeman, in September. "The death rate is over one hundred every day. The undertakers can't bury them fast enough. We find a lot that have been dead three or four days. My God it is fearful."

On September 12 the *Appeal* reported that the "handsome German woman" Annie Cook, madam of the Mansion House, "who had ventured all she had of life and property for the sick [,] died yesterday at 7 o'clock of yellow fever." Late in September, businessman Charles G. Fisher wrote, just before he died: "Our city is a hospital. Fifteen volunteer physicians have died—two others sick. Many nurses have died. We are praying for frost. It is our only hope."

It came the morning of October 19. Residents who began returning later in October found a town still haunted by the specter of death. Whole families had disappeared so that no one was left to say how to dispose of their property. Estimates of the economic losses in the Mississippi Valley ran to one hundred million dollars. Total deaths in Memphis had reached 5,150, and among whites the mortality rate had been seventy percent. By any measure, it was one of the three worst epidemics ever experienced by a Southern city.

The board of Union and Planters met, for the first time in two and a half months, on November 4, 1878. Some means had to be found to reward the officers who had protected the stockholders' interests throughout the epidemic. But the board had trouble deciding on the proper course. After discussing the question for a month, they finally presented the officers with this resolution of tribute:

Whereas a terrible Scourge in the shape of a yellow fever epidemic having recently invaded our beautiful City carrying in its mad career death and destruction to every home, making thousands of Widows and Orphans, visiting alike every class, exempting none: its progress and march being more terrible than an army with banners—

And whereas a few of the noble and brave having in their charge and keeping important trusts, remained at their posts discharging every duty and trust confided to them with honour and fidelity, rendering a faithful and satisfactory account of every matter intrusted to their care and keeping—

And whereas those of the officers and employees of the Union & Planters Bank who remained at their posts during the terrible Scourge performing every duty with great promptness and fidelity in each department intrusted to them—

Resolved by the Board of Directors of the Union and Planters Bank at its meeting this the 11th day of December 1878 that the thanks of this Board are due and hereby tendered and the highest praise awarded to this truly brave and noble band of officers and employees, who thus remained at their posts performing every duty necessary to the protection and interest of this Bank.

Resolved as another and more substantial evidence of our high appreciation, confidence and esteem for the officers and employees of this Bank who thus remained, that we directors authorize and instruct the Cashier of this bank to pay to the president and cashier double salary for the months of September and October and double salary for the said two months to all employees who remained at their post during the entire months of September and October, and also to the widow of the late Louis Czapski two months double salary.

And be it further Resolved that as the late Louis Czapski of this noble band of faithful employees has been taken from us, called from his labors on earth to serve his Father in Heaven, it is the sense of the Board in the death of Louis Czapski this Bank has lost one of its most useful faithful and efficient employees, whose zeal and fidelity to its interests were well known and appreciated by this Board, and the community at large has lost a true man and useful citizen—So to the bereaved family this Board hereby tenders their heartfelt sympathy in this their great sorrow. Resolved. That these proceedings be spread upon the minutes of the Bank as a testimonial of the high esteem and appreciation of this Board for those of its officers and employees who thus imperiled life itself in the interest of the Bank, and the Cashier be instructed to forward a copy of the same to the widow of the late Louis Czapski.

One last tribute was left to pay. On Christmas Day of 1878, the bank's stockholders gathered in the boardroom. R. Dudley Frayser, lawyer and financier, spoke for them all when he told Samuel Read:

A number of your friends, stockholders of this bank, have thought it proper that they should present you some token of their esteem for you as a man. . . .

The position you have occupied in this bank since its birth has been filled by you in a manner that reflects the highest credit upon you as an officer of superior merit. . . . While your official relations have been such as to elicit the entire approval of the stockholders, they feel there was a time when your fidelity and faithfulness to your trust was more praiseworthy and far more commendable than is that care and attention you are called on to bestow upon your duties in ordinary times. . . .

To face death on the field amid the clangor of arms, and to die amid the clamor and plaudits of one's comrades, is an easy thing; but to remain at the post of duty, when the air is filled by an unseen enemy and a dire contagion is daily carrying to the grave hundreds of those who remain in an desolated city, this, sir, is the loftiest art of heroism. For nearly three months you did this, and against the entreaties and prayers of your friends, your wife, and your children, remained and kept the doors of this institution open, thereby enabling the many benevolent organizations to raise money with which to relieve the distress of a stricken and impoverished people. Had you faltered, this bank would have closed and the hand of charity been thereby paralyzed for want of an avenue to reach the needy, and this bank's prestige would have to some extent been lowered.

Citing the custom of presenting a memento to the "brave and the true," Frayser gave Read a five-hundred dollar watch, and said: "Accept this watch, and may its mechanism prove as true to its object as you have to your trust; and when it shall no longer for you mark the flight of time, may you at the hands of the Giver of all good gifts receive the reward that attends upon a wellspent life."

Read's words of acceptance were plainspoken, less ornate than Frayser's. "Gentlemen," he said, "Upon no occasion in life have I been more highly gratified and flattered than upon this one. The remarks of your speaker, Colonel Frayser, are eloquent and concerning me very complimentary. He commends me highly for fidelity in the performance of duty during the epidemic. It was, gentlemen, only the performance of a very plain and simple duty; nevertheless, a very imperative one—a debt, it might be called, that could not be repudiated—a debt of honor. . . . This handsome and valuable gift is most thankfully accepted, and will ever be valued as a testimonial of your approval."

After the Yellow Fever

And both of his parents were also Memphis to the core. Their forefathers had lived there, as the local saying was, since before the Yellow Fever.
—Peter Taylor, *A Summons to Memphis*

FOR MEMPHIS the yellow fever of 1878 was what the Civil War was for many other southern cities—a time marker like B.C. People dated from it. One historian ventures to say that after the 1878 epidemic "a second metropolis . . . sprang up . . . on the ruins of the first." Certainly Memphis in the winter of 1878 did look like a fallen world to most residents, and they were ready to apply desperate remedies.

Before the epidemic the *Appeal,* voicing popular sentiment, had come out against the businessmen's proposal to repeal the city charter. Afterwards the public's view changed and so did the *Appeal*'s. "This present visitation is the straw on the camel's back," wrote editor Keating. "We can endure no more. We must have relief from ignorance and incompetency in government, [and] the cormorant greed of city and foreign creditors."

Napoleon Hill, E. M. Apperson and their associates in the People's Protective Union saw the opening they had looked for since 1875. On New Year's Eve they organized a citizens' meeting that ended with the crowd calling for surrender of the city charter and repudiation of all or part of the city's debt. Less than two weeks later, the Board of Aldermen, feeling the weight of public opinion bearing down on them, passed a resolution asking the state legislature to take back the charter granted Memphis in 1826; on January 31, 1879 the legislature complied, revoking home rule in the Bluff City.

Legally, Memphis was no more. In its place was a state-controlled entity called the Taxing District of Shelby County, administered by a board of local businessmen appointed by the governor. The Protective Union thereby attained its aims of "cheap government and low taxes," of driving the "damn theives" from city hall, and of putting a stop to the court-ordered collections by its creditors. In return the city had politically reverted to a quasi-territory, governed by overseers appointed in Nashville.

It was a drastic step. Old J. J. Rawlings, who had arrived in Memphis before its incorporation, commented sadly: "I have outlived the city. It has forfeited its charter, and I am still here." Although a great many Southern cities were also in deep financial trouble, only two others—Mobile and Selma, Alabama—would follow Memphis down the road to municipal suicide.

Already reputed to be a pest hole deadlier than New Orleans, Memphis also became a financial leper in the eyes of Northern capitalists when it offered to settle with city bondholders at 33⅓ cents on the dollar. A "scandalous act of dishonesty . . . adopted to enable Memphis to rob its creditors," stormed the *New York Times,* calling the partial repudiation the act of a city "insensitive to shame. No city has ever descended so low in financial infamy."

While bankers such as Napoleon Hill had planned and executed this "infamy," they were able to distance themselves from it. That was fortunate for Memphis, because its commerce and banking depended on seasonal loans from Northern and upper Mid-western banks. During the peak cotton harvesting and marketing months of fall and early winter, the local demand for money—reflected in bank clearings—would jump to about $3.5 million a week by the late 1880s, as compared to around $2.5 million weekly during the quieter months.[1] Memphis banks, not having the resources to meet those long surges of demand, had to borrow from their correspondents in the larger money centers, primarily New York, Chicago, Cincinnati, and St. Louis. If those banks refused to lend, the result could be a panic and depression such as the one in 1873.

Union and Planters' access to Northern money markets continued despite the hard feelings over partial repudiation. This was largely owing to the close relationships the cashier and some of the directors had formed with a few influential Wall Street financiers. On March 25, 1879, Read wired the board from New York: "Deposited $150,000 with Central Trust Company, on demand, 3 percent interest. Bought $200,000 1040s, 1 3/8 premium, instead of lending, by approval and advise of wise friends including Cossitt."

The wise friend named Cossitt was Frederick H. Cossitt, a Connecticut Yankee who had migrated to Memphis in 1842 to amass his first fortune in trading. Along the way he made the acquaintance of Robertson Topp, William Farrington, Samuel Read, and Napoleon Hill. A few months before the Civil War broke out, Cossitt returned north, but kept in touch with his circle of business acquaintances in Memphis, sometimes acting as their go-between in transactions with large Northern merchant banks. In April 1864, for instance, Cossitt persuaded Brown Brothers [now Brown Brothers Harriman] to lend Robertson Topp substantial sums on the strength of a permit Topp was then angling to obtain from President Lincoln empowering him to travel freely across Federal lines and trade in cotton.[2] After Cossitt's death in 1887, his heirs donated seventy-five thousand dollars toward the construction of Memphis' first public library, whose original board of trustees included Samuel Read, William Farrington, and Napoleon Hill.

The advice of wise friends such as Cossitt helped Union and Planters to continue turning profits even though the depression had not yet lifted in the South. Past due notes in July 1880 totaled $22,305, nearly half of which were the doubtful Farrington-Greenlaw notes. In July the board reduced dividends from five to four percent, though earnings for the past six months had risen slightly above the usual figure, to $37,331.

At the start of 1881, as business conditions improved, the bank unexpectedly lost its president. On February 22, Samuel Read called the directors together and told them that C. W. Goyer had died at eleven o'clock that morning. That news moved them to adopt a resolution that shows a depth of feeling seldom if ever equalled in later memorials:

> Mr. Goyer was identified with this bank from its organization, and served as a director until January, 1874, when he became its president, and so continued . . . until this day. It was proper that it should be so, for he was honest and capable, fearless and faithful. Only afraid to do wrong, he stood by his trust through every vicissitude, that he might do his whole duty. A good man has gone to rest. His chair on the board shall be draped for thirty days, but long after that his loss will be deplored by the directory.

Goyer had been ill for some months, but he seemed indestructible, and the directors had not thought out who would succeed him. At their meeting on March 2, someone nominated Vice-president Williamson, and the board elected him president. Williamson thanked them for the honor, but reminding them that he lived in Brownsville and could not stay in Memphis several days a week, he "declined to serve." Trying again, the directors nominated and elected long, lean Allison C. Treadwell. Treadwell accepted the office and, deciding to work at it full time, retired from the cotton firm he owned in partnership with his younger brother, Arthur. Before adjourning, the directors filled Goyer's chair on the board with Samuel Read.

By 1883 Memphis had begun to repair some of the damage done during the 1870s by "disease, debt, and municipal corruption". Although Mark Twain rightly observed that the city streets were still "not paved in a way to incite distempered admiration," Memphis had constructed a sewer system, and other reforms were in progress: garbage collection, plumbing regulation, birth registration, meat and milk inspection, compulsory vaccination for smallpox, and a pure water system. The Taxing District increased the rate of settlement on municipal bonds from 33⅓ cents to 50 cents on the dollar, which allowed most bondholders to clear a one hundred percent profit, since they had purchased the bonds at an average price of 25 cents on the dollar. Those who held out could expect an even greater profit later on.

Furthermore, a few businessmen were attempting to add some much-needed diversity to the local economy. Aside from the cotton-oil industry, manufacturing was all but non-existent. Cotton, like ivory going from the Congo to Europe, flowed by the tons from Memphis to the mills of New England—then returned as clothing. Economically locked into a colonial relationship with the North, Memphis exported raw materials and imported finished goods.

The gospel of the cotton mill as salvation from the rigors of Reconstruction had caught on in towns throughout the South, notably in Georgia and the Carolinas. But the cotton mill gospel failed to take hold in Memphis and the Delta, where life revolved around the soil rather than the machine (the new business year began with the cotton harvest in September, and most debts to tradesmen were set to mature as the cotton came to market). The first post-war attempt to spin and knit cotton locally had been made by Napoleon Hill, William Williamson, and a former director of

Union and Planters, John Johnson. With a $40,000 loan from Union and Planters, the Pioneer Mill had opened in 1882. Pioneer eventually proved unprofitable and was shut down, but Hill went on to invest in other projects that held promise of lending balance to the economy. Hill, Read, and T. J. Latham—a Union and Planters director from 1884 to 1885—organized the Chickasaw Land Company in 1887. An early example of an industrial development park, Chickasaw offered manufacturers free sites, water, low taxes, and railroad connections on its 3,175-acre property.

Hill could easily afford to take a few chances on cotton mills, industrial parks, coal lands in Alabama, even a local stove factory. His genius for trading—"bull luck" he called it—seldom deserted him. In news articles he was often referred to as the "merchant prince of the South." Hill, Fontaine Company, with its newly opened St. Louis branch run by brother Jerome Hill, was the third largest cotton house in the world, grossing some $5.5 million annually. On top of that there were the steady dividends from Hill's insurance companies, his cotton compress and warehouse company, his commercial real estate holdings, and his interests in banks, railroads, and utilities. Hill's estate, after liberal gifts to his wife and three children, would contain admitted assets worth $1.758 million, in the hard and income tax-free money of 1909.[3]

While playing his favorite card game, euchre, Hill might forget himself and spit tobacco juice on his hostess's fine oriental rug, and sometimes he might take his first drink a little before his usual time of two o'clock, but such quirks were accepted as normal for so expansive a character. Anyway, there was not yet enough genuinely "old" money in town for people to make snide remarks about the bumptiousness of the newly rich.

If Hill liked anything more than making money it was spending it. "I am able and want my children to have everything that will add to their comfort and pleasure," he wrote his wife in 1885. "I do not expect to take any of my fortune with me when I die, and there are none that I love more than my own family and I want them to enjoy it. . . . So *don't* stint yourself but get everything you need."[4]

Enjoy it they did. On the northeast corner of Third and Madison, workmen built Hill a sprawling Second Empire mansion that bristled with towers, cupolas, and other rococo details. The master bedroom was Hill's particular joy. Its furnishings included a prize-winning bedroom suite that Hill had spotted on display at the 1876 Centennial Exposition in Philadelphia. The suite hadn't been for sale, but no matter. Hill had to have it, and he persuaded officials to let him buy this treasure. It was indeed fit for a merchant prince of the Gilded Age, its "dark walnut inlaid with a variety of oddly grained woods, painted and stained in many colors from gilt to lamp black, carved and curled intricately."[5]

In their Xanadu on the Mississippi, the Hill's entertained regally. "Champagne flowed like water," reported one guest, "and tropical fruits bloomed on the table in the sear month of November."[6]

Hill never claimed to be a philanthropist or civic benefactor, but his expansive nature did prompt a certain open-handedness in business matters where Memphis stood to gain. An opportunity of that sort arose in the summer of 1885. The proposition was put to Hill by one of his cronies, David P. "Pappy" Hadden, who had served as president of the Taxing District for three years. Like Napoleon Hill, Pappy Hadden would never have been mistaken for a squire from the Virginia Tidewater. A feisty Irishman, Hadden presided over city court as though on a vaudeville stage, cracking jokes, leading witnesses into making comic statements, and closing each session by telling his appreciative audience: "The performance is over. Don't be late tomorrow, there are no reserved seats." He rode about town on his mule, Hulda, and to reduce his court docket he invented a curious device known as the Hadden horn, which was designed to guarantee an honest roll of the dice.

Hadden also was given credit for pushing through many of the health and sanitary reforms that were making the city look less and less like a poor borough in sixteenth century London. What he now wanted from Napoleon Hill was a loan from Union and Planters to help retire the last of the city's debt.

At Hill's invitation, Hadden put his case before the directors at their meeting of June 11. Hadden explained that the Taxing District had reached agreement with the owner of the majority of outstanding bonds to settle at seventy percent of face value. To raise the necessary seven hundred thousand dollars, the Taxing District intended to issue thirty-year bonds, which would be easier to sell if Memphis investors took the first two hundred thousand dollars of the issue. The Bank of Commerce and the First National, said Hadden, had each pledged to take twenty thousand dollars of the issue. Not since 1871 had the board considered buying so much as twenty cents of Memphis bonds. But after talking over the proposition the directors voted to buy twenty-five thousand dollars worth. Although the Taxing District had its drawbacks, at least it had enabled government and business to cooperate again after more than two decades of mutual recriminations.

As relations warmed with city hall, relations among the directors themselves grew chilly. How the ill-feelings originated and eventually split the
board is unclear. But through one or another series of disagreements, President Treadwell and Cashier Read arrived at a standoff. Neither could work
with the other. On August 8, 1885, a Saturday, the directors met in adjourned session to consider a complaint Treadwell had drawn up against
Read, charging him with "irregularity or wrong." Specifically, Treadwell
said that the cashier had permitted Theodore Read, his son, to use the
bank's bond trading account to Theodore's profit and the bank's loss.
Treadwell asked the board to censure Read. Deciding to sift the evidence
carefully before passing judgment, the board created an investigative committee composed of Williamson, Hill, Bruce, and two new directors, Isaac
N. Snowden and R. Dudley Frayser.

The committeemen took their time, perhaps hoping that time would
bring Treadwell and Read to a compromise. But Read was no compro-
miser; a man of fixed opinions, blunt, even caustic when angered, he demanded vindication. Treadwell, equally certain of himself, insisted that the
board act.

The committeemen presented their findings on October 1. They had in-
terviewed both Treadwell and Read, queried a bank in New York, and
asked the opinions of officials at three Memphis banks. Their judgment
was that Theodore Read had committed irregularities but without his father's knowledge, that Union and Planters had lost nothing in the process,
and that other Memphis banks often approved similar transactions. While
mincing no words, the committee asked Treadwell and Read to put aside
their differences in the interest of harmony:

> We do not think that this [series of bond transactions] ought to be
> perverted into an irregularity. . . . We are satisfied no reflection can
> be cast upon the Cashier. We believe, both Mr. Treadwell and
> Mr. Read desire to render the Bank efficient aid, and their attachment
> for an Institution for which they have so long labored, should be
> an incentive for them to work harmoniously for the good of the
> Bank.

For both men, however, what had been done could not be forgotten. Before the day was over Treadwell sold his Union and Planters stock and sent
the directors his resignation, thanking them "for any courtesy or aid that
may have been extended to me during my official career."[7] Within the

week two more directors, W. B. Galbreath and J. F. Frank, also sold their stock and departed.

(Time erased the bitterness left by the quarrel, though not in Treadwell or Read's generation. In 1966, William D. Galbreath, W. B.'s grandson, joined the bank's board. And in 1971, Timmons L. Treadwell, great-great-nephew of Allison C. Treadwell, was elected a director.)

Samuel Read's position at Union and Planters henceforth was well nigh impregnable; never again in his lifetime would anyone seriously challenge his authority. Significantly, it was Read whom the directors asked to nominate the next president. He was "truly glad" for that privilege, he told them. "I will name one that has been a Director from [the] beginning, and one every way worthy and eminently satisfactory to each and every member of this directory, and I nominate Mr. Napoleon Hill." The directors, acting in concord once again, unanimously elected Hill president.

The opening years of Napoleon Hill's administration brought the longest stretch of stability and prosperity the bank had seen. From 1885 to 1890, profits consistently ranged from $80,000 to $90,000 yearly. Dividends rose to six percent. Overdrafts and past due notes were held to a negligible fraction of total loans, which hardly varied—from $1 million to $1.5 million, depending on the season. Deposits increased from $820,466 to $1.233 million. In December 1887, and again in June 1888, when the State of Tennessee asked to borrow funds with which to meet interest payments on its bonds, Union and Planters loaned the money requested.[8] The bank's condition, in the words of the examining committee, was "most sound, solvent, and prosperous."

Toward the end of 1889, however, there were hints of rougher going ahead. As early as January the directors had noticed a "stagnation" of commerce. That slow-down soon affected the Chickasaw Land Company's capacity to pay its note on schedule; in May the board granted Chickasaw a two-year extension. At the same time, the bank's deposits and loans stopped growing, while those of the State National Bank and the Bank of Commerce continued to increase year by year. Since 1869, Union and Planters had been Memphis' big bank by nearly any measure: deposits, capital, loans. That was no longer the case in 1889. The Bank of Commerce had pulled ahead in capital, deposits, and loans. Two other banks, the State National and the German, were also on the move; the resources of each were now only slightly less than those held by Union and Planters.

Not only was competition on the rise but Union and Planters was losing directors to its competitors. E. M. Apperson had left to join the board of the German Bank. T. J. Latham went to the State National, and R. Dudley Frayser resigned to accept the presidency of the Security Bank. President Hill stayed, but his thoughts often drifted back into the past. He experienced the nostalgia of the elderly, a yearning to go back and re-capture the days of his youth. In April 1889, when the board approved his request for a sixty-day leave of absence, Hill and his favorite daughter, Olivia, set off for California to visit what remained of the mining camps and boom towns Hill had known so well.

The great depression of the 1890s is said to have started with the Panic of 1893. In the North, no sharp downturn was felt until May 1893. In the South, however, the depression was well underway by 1891. That year the proportion of business failures in the South was as high as it would go in 1893. Interest rates rose, prices fell. Ten pounds of cotton had earned a farmer one dollar in 1870; to earn a dollar in 1890 he needed fifteen pounds. Squeezed between eight-cent cotton and ten-percent mortgages, thousands of farmers would soon be share-cropping on the land they had once owned.

The agricultural crisis had little effect on Memphis at first. In 1891 the city regained its charter and home rule, having gotten out from under the crushing load of municipal debt. The same year construction began on the "Great Bridge," which would span the Mississippi at Memphis. When completed in 1892 it was the third largest bridge in the world, and the only railroad bridge across the Mississippi south of St. Louis. Freight to and from the lower West would henceforth move faster and more efficiently.

By then the depression in the countryside was beginning to spill over into Memphis. On July 5, 1892, Union and Planters lowered dividends to five percent. The reduction came of prudence rather than of necessity, but one director and several customers were less fortunate. With an overdrawn account and notes past due, Director Isaac Snowden gave up his seat on the board. His house had been taken by creditors and was scheduled to be auctioned in August.

William Farrington, now a vice-president of the Continental Bank, was also caught short. He had "hypothecated," or pledged as collateral, all that he owned but still found himself "embarrassed," which was to say unable to pay what he owed. Farrington had fallen behind in paying several thousand dollars he owed Union and Planters. When the bank called his loan, Farrington "pleaded" with the board of Continental Bank for a loan of ten thousand dollars. The directors frowned on this plan to borrow from Peter to pay Paul, especially since they were already carrying past due notes for Vice-President Farrington. They turned him down, whereupon he told them that if they refused him "he would be very seriously embarrassed, and that on account of his being vice-president of the bank [its directors and the bank] would be very greatly embarrassed." They still turned him down.[9]

Economic conditions worsened in 1894, probably the darkest year the nation had seen since the Civil War. Coxey's "army" of the jobless marched on Washington in the spring. Bloody strikes broke out at the Pullman factories in Chicago and in coal mining towns in Alabama and Tennessee. The price of cotton in Memphis dropped to an all-time low of four and one-half cents a pound. Adding to the worries of Memphis businessmen were reports that out in the impoverished cotton lands the Farmers' Alliance was gaining support for free coinage of silver an end to the gold standard.

It was during this year of trouble and alarms, in November, that a small blood vessel ruptured inside the head of Napoleon Hill. The stroke left his intelligence and memory unimpaired, but he often had to grope for the right word to express his thoughts. There were awkward silences at board meetings as Hill struggled to find words. It angered and depressed him that his mind was full of ideas which his tongue could no longer say. His aphasia proved irreversible, but he stayed on as president of Union and Planters. Even after a second stroke partially paralyzed him in January 1896, he continued in office. For all practical purposes, though, the duties of president were taken up by Samuel Read. In January 1897 the board made that transfer of authority official, electing Read president.

Napoleon Hill lived for twelve years longer, an invalid confined to his enormous gilded bed. Gradually his mansion and his money became less real to him than his memories of the California gold fields. He told and retold stories about gold-crazed forty-niners, about wagon trains bound for California, and pretty senoritas in the pale moonlight. His wife listened to the stories. Often, she remembered, "it would take him minutes to formulate and utter a single word."

CHAPTER 5

Mr. Read's Bank

*The banker can well say that eternal vig-
ilance is the price of the life of the bank.*
—Samuel P. Read (1910)

THIRTY-FIVE years spent watching the shifting fortunes of Memphis
businessmen had not made an optimist or a diplomat of Samuel Read.
Those who knew him considered him "one of the most conservative
bankers in the South," and in that as in most other matters Read seldom left
anybody in doubt about his views. His readiness to speak bluntly, even to
the great and powerful, was well known. Businessmen sometimes would
stop by Union and Planters for no other reason than to see if they could
loosen his sharp tongue.

One subject that often drew his withering comments was overchecking.
The overdrawn account, he liked to say,

is one evil almost local to Memphis, even to mention which might be
resented as an unauthorized interference with the vested rights of
bank customers and cause many of them to say, 'Look at Read again
on his hobby [horse]. . . . Some customers are so impressed with
their right to overcheck at pleasure that a notice, even a mention of it,
would be resented. On this subject competition has made us all cow-
ards, but nevertheless I have made a hard fight against the evil. Un-

less the banker does make this fight he will soon be without money and without securities, and will have nothing to take to New York to pledge as collateral except his overcheck book.

Another thou-shalt-not involved the opening of accounts. No account was to be accepted unless the new customer produced the endorsement of an established customer, who thereby agreed to make good any loss to Union and Planters. It was a rule without exceptions, and had been followed for many years, ever since "a wealthy customer seemed to take much pride in introducing his friend from Philadelphia, and somewhat resented the requirement of his endorsement to get the $40.00 draft of his friend cashed. A week later our collector called on him and got his check to reimburse us for the draft [that had been] returned protested for non-payment, which valuable paper we hear is still among the archives of the family."

Lending policy also emphasized security above other considerations. "A banker must not furnish capital," Read maintained. He believed that commercial banks had no business granting accommodation loans; that is, long-term credits used to make capital improvements. The bank might extend the credit a merchant needed to stock his shelves for a season, but not to build a warehouse or a cotton gin. These trade loans, maturing in a year or sooner, allowed a quick return and minimized exposure to economic downturns. As Read put it, "commercial banks are intended to move the wheels of commerce by dealing in short time paper, thereby always having their funds as nearly as possible at command to meet the demands of trade and the calls of depositors. Fixed and long time paper paralyzes, and too much of it shuts the doors of the bank, and it would be said the bank died of slow assets."[1]

By limiting the scope of transactions and holding customers strictly accountable, President Read very nearly swept the books clean of bad paper. Earnings accumulated and dividend payments went out twice yearly without fail. There were no surprises to vex the directors. Naturally, however, the tight controls limited growth. Deposits, totalling $1.332 million in 1900, had increased hardly at all since 1896, and loan volume remained fairly constant year in and year out.

While growth at Union and Planters leveled off, just the opposite was happening among its competitors. The Bank of Commerce, organized mainly by Robert Bogardus Snowden, had opened in 1873 with one-third the capital stock of Union and Planters; by 1904 its capital stock, resources, and deposits had increased to twice the size of those on hand at Union and Planters. The First National was on the move as well, its deposits having risen from $750,000 to $1.05 million after it bought the German Bank in 1897. Moreover, several banks of recent origin were prospering in fields ignored by their strictly commercial counterparts. They rented safe-deposit boxes, sometimes specialized in mortgage lending, and frequently sold securities, fire insurance, and surety bonds; but primarily they concentrated on one or both of the promising new fields in banking: savings deposits and trust services.

Interest-bearing accounts were unknown in Memphis during the Civil War and for almost a generation thereafter. Not until 1885 did post-war Memphis see its first savings bank, the Manhattan Savings and Trust Company, whose founders included Napoleon Hill. Slow though it was to develop, the concept of interest-bearing accounts had caught on rapidly after 1885. During the next six years, eight other savings banks went into business, so that by 1892 half of the city's banks offered accounts paying three or four percent interest. As early as 1892 the nine savings banks had attracted more than twenty thousand depositors and claimed $1.4 million of the total $9 million on deposit with Memphis banks.

Equally striking was the rise of trust companies. Through the 1860s and '70s state laws had preserved the distinction between the fiduciary functions of trust companies and the money lending, deposit taking business of banks. In the 1880s, however, the legal barriers came down, and hybrid corporations that combined elements of both began to appear. Commercial banks faced still another rival, for the trust companies could accept checking and savings accounts, and they could lend. The enactment of Tennessee's first inheritance tax, in 1891, undoubtedly helped increase their popularity. Between 1898 and 1903, no less than thirty-eight trust companies opened in Tennessee.

One of them, the Tennessee Trust Company in Memphis, was of particular interest to the board of Union and Planters. Initially called the Security Bank of Memphis, it had been formed in 1886 by R. Dudley Frayser, who had resigned as a director of Union and Planters in order to head the Security Bank. From the beginning Frayser's trust company and Union and Planters had interlocking directorates. William Williamson, John R. Pepper and, for a while, Samuel Read held board seats or offices in both companies. Pepper, who became president of the Goyer Company after the death of C. W. Goyer, had joined the bank's board in 1885. In 1903 Pepper was president of Tennessee Trust and first vice-president of Union and

Planters. Under him Tennessee Trust was "noted for its rapid growth and enterprising spirit." By 1904 it had attracted deposits of $1.305, or roughly forty percent of the total funds on deposit with Union and Planters.

The advantages likely to result from merging the two corporations had apparently been discussed off and on since at least 1903. The talking stage ended in March 1906 when the joint boards announced that on May 1 their interests would be consolidated under the name of Union and Planters Bank and Trust Company. In addition to the change of name, the bank changed its headquarters, moving across the alley to the modern and spacious quarters of the fifteen-story Tennessee Trust Building, which then was the tallest building in Memphis.

By means of the consolidation, Union and Planters became Memphis' first "department store bank," offering the full range of services, from mortgage loans and trusts to savings accounts, stock and bond brokerage, and safe-deposit vaults. It could handle not only more lines of business but larger lines. With resources of $6.921 million, capital stock of $1.4 million, and deposits approaching $5 million, the bank was now the second largest in Memphis, after the Bank of Commerce.[2]

The consolidation also brought nine new directors to the board. Three were cotton factors: W. E. Gage, J. M. McCormack, and Frank M. Norfleet. Two developed real estate: J. F. Holst and B. Lee Mallory, president of the South Memphis Land Company, successor to the Chickasaw Land Company. There was a merchant, Harry Cohn of Dixie Clothing; a manufacturer, Henry Winkelman of Winkelman Baking Company; and a banker, James F. Hunter, who had charge of the savings department.

And there was Guston T. Fitzhugh, an attorney who was named counsel to the bank. Fiercely combative in and out of court, Fitzhugh was a leader in the increasingly powerful anti-saloon movement and a perennial champion of other controversial causes.[3] When his friend, the brilliant and brash prohibitionist Edward Ward Carmack, was killed in a gun battle fought on the streets of Nashville in 1909, Fitzhugh volunteered to assist in prosecuting the two wet Democrats charged with the slaying. He called them "assassins" and demanded the death penalty, but the evidence suggested that Carmack had fired the first shot, and the jury returned a verdict of second degree murder. Fitzhugh would play a critical part in the re-organization of Union and Planters in the 1920s.

The ten-year expansion of the money supply in Memphis came to a full stop in the autumn of 1907. The cause, as in 1893 and 1873, was financial panic on Wall Street, touched off by the failure on October 23 of the Knickerbocker Bank. When New York's large banks cut off credit to their correspondents in the West and South, the panic spread. Currency disappeared from circulation in much of the South.

Samuel Read, president of the Memphis Clearinghouse Association, took steps on October 28 to protect local banks from a run by their worried depositors. In accordance with the plan devised by Read and adopted by the Clearinghouse, banks restricted their customers to one hundred dollars in withdrawals a day, and in an effort to bring money out of hiding, the restriction was waived on new deposits.

Pressure on the banks eased, but trade suffered from the lack of ready cash. The *Commercial Appeal* reported that friends were beginning to start conversations with each other by asking, "What are you using for money?"

On November 7, in a meeting at the Memphis Businessmen's Club, Samuel Read and other bankers convinced some two hundred merchants that the only way out was for them to accept "cashier's checks," or scrip, printed up by the bankers in small denominations and payable to "Jno. Doe or bearer." This emergency money, though later ruled illegal by the United States Secretary of the Treasury, kept business moving by restoring purchasing power to thousands of wage earners whose payroll checks had been negotiable only at a ruinous discount, if at all.

While it lasted, the Panic of 1907 caused acute distress, but it didn't lead to years of depression such as had followed the Panics of 1893 and 1873. Conditions returned to normal in the spring of 1908, and the monetary crisis was forgotten as Memphians turned their attention to the stir kicked up by one of their new fire and police commissioners, a tall, red-headed young man named Edward Hull Crump. Born in Holly Springs, Mississippi, Crump had come to Memphis in 1894, attained moderate success in business, and then discovered that his true calling—and genius—lay in politics.

Campaigning on a reform ticket, Crump had won a fire and police post despite the opposition of the powerful Walsh-Malone faction, and in one of his first official acts he staged a dramatic crackdown on gambling houses that had supported the Walsh-Malone ticket. Soon after that he was front-page news again: through intensive and well-publicized lobbying he secured passage of a legislative act that changed city government from the council to the commission form, which was widely thought to be a step toward more efficient and progressive government.

To no one's great surprise, Crump then declared his candidacy for mayor in the commission government to be elected in November 1909. His chances appeared slim to most political observers, who knew that his opponent, ex-mayor Joe Williams, was still popular and had the backing of the Walsh-Malone organization. The campaign turned out to be a milestone in Memphis' history, and it also produced a landmark in American music.

Crump's supporters, looking for a theme song that would appeal to black voters, commissioned a song from composer and bandleader William Christopher Handy. The result, "Mr. Crump," was the first published arrangement of Blues music. With new lyrics and re titled "The Memphis Blues (Or, Mr. Crump)," the song launched Handy's career as a nationally known musician. It may even have influenced the mayor's race, for out of the 11,713 ballots cast, Crump was elected by the slender margin of 75 votes.

Once in office, Crump built a political organization that was to assure his political mastery of city and county government until his death forty-five years later. In time he won nearly unanimous approval from businessmen, and according to his official biographer, "it came to be almost the first rule of sound business procedure to support the [Crump] organization. It was even more; it was a mark of status signifying that a businessman's values were in order."[4] Crump gave Memphis efficient government and low taxes in exchange for the freedom to employ whatever methods he thought necessary to maintain his political power. As a friend and close associate of his later explained: "He bribed the people with good government."[5]

A great many Memphians might not have known exactly what to expect from Ed Crump, but in 1912 most of them believed that after fifty years of political isolation the South had at last found a standard bearer in President-elect Woodrow Wilson. Between 1861 and Wilson's inauguration, no Southerner except Andrew Johnson had served as President or Vice-president; of the 133 cabinet officers named during that period, only 14 had been from the South. For all practical purposes the region was "as effectively cut off from all influence in the management of the United States Government as it would be if it was a British Crown colony," remarked one U.S. Senator.

Wilson's victory put some Memphians in mind of the rising fortunes the South experienced after the elections of Thomas Jefferson and Andrew Jackson. Bands played *Dixie!* at Wilson's inauguration, and five of his ten cabinet officers were from below the Potomac.

During his first year in office Wilson threw his support behind several reforms of benefit to the region. The most important was the formation of the Federal Reserve System, designed to protect the banking system against financial panics resulting from temporary shortages of money. As originally drafted, the plan called for a single reserve bank located in the North. But the Wilson Administration and Virginia Senator Carter Glass, thinking that enough financial power was already concentrated in the Northeast, succeeded in providing for the creation of regional reserve banks as well. No longer was Wall Street the sole lender of last resort in an emergency.

Southerners, and Southern farmers in particular, also welcomed the tariff revision of 1913. Under the Morrill Tariff, enacted in 1861, duty on imported goods had climbed from eighteen to forty-seven percent. The tariff favored manufacturers, located mostly in the Northeast, over farmers in the West and South. Protected from foreign competition, manufacturers collaborated in setting up trusts to fix the prices farmers paid for fertilizer, barbed wire, shoes, and other necessities. It made government, said Wilson, "a facile instrument in the hands of private interests." Congress sharply reduced the tariff in 1913, despite the protests of manufacturers.

Although the South was not exactly rising again, it was experiencing a resurgence. Perhaps at no other time since 1858 had the region's prospects looked better than they did in the summer of 1914. Cotton production was rising and, for a change, so were prices. A bumper crop, estimated to be the largest ever, was ripening. Brokers confidently placed its total value at one billion dollars or more.

The sense of security, however, changed to extreme uncertainty when news arrived that war had broken out in Europe. Cotton immediately fell off ten dollars a bale. The Memphis Cotton Exchange failed to open on August 3; other major exchanges, in New Orleans and Galveston, also remained closed. In some Delta towns the price dropped below five cents a pound. A nationwide campaign to "bale out the South" started in October, with retailers such as Gimbel Brothers urging their customers to "buy a bale" of raw cotton at ten cents a pound. The market stabilized somewhat in November as large orders from England were received. But for the next six years the demand for Memphis' chief product would undergo dizzying fluctuations not seen since the 1860s.

His career had spanned half a century, from the Civil War to the World War, from the age of wildcat banking to that of the Federal Reserve System. At age eighty-three, Samuel Read was the oldest banker still active in Memphis, and probably one of the few octogenarians running a sizable bank anywhere in the nation. Failing eyesight and other maladies had troubled him for some time, but never enough to tempt him into retirement. In his old man's body there remained the fierce devotion to Union and Planters.

Even after his health broke early in January 1915, Read carried on the duties of president almost to the last. There were days when he insisted, against his doctor's advice, on going to the bank. No urgent business required his presence, but he went all the same.

By the end of January, Read could no longer venture from his house, which was on the bluff, at the corner of South Front and Pontotoc, where he had settled when it was among the best addresses in Memphis, and where he had stayed as, one by one, most of his well-to-do neighbors had migrated eastward and as their mansions were boarded up or razed or turned into apartment houses. From his home in the decaying neighborhood, Read kept check on the bank. Each day, Gilmer Winston or another officer, following Read's instructions, would bring him a statement of the bank's condition, which he is reported to have "inquired closely into," until satisfied that all was still in order. These daily examinations continued up to February 4, when Read slipped into a coma. He died shortly before midnight four days later.

The "Dean of Memphis Bankers," as the *Commercial Appeal* called him in a front-page obituary, had stood his watch with the unremitting vigilance that, according to his favorite maxim, was "the price of the life of the bank." His exacting judgments of what constituted financial value were generally held to be almost as safe as gold. "Hundreds and hundreds of Memphians," the *Commercial Appeal* reported, "are familiar with the little endorsement, 'S. P. R.' When it finally went on a piece of commercial paper, that paper seldom went bad."

"A Gentleman to the Manner Born"

Business is friendship.
—slogan of Union and Planters Bank (1919)

THE turnover of sixteen directors in seven years had all but eliminated the old guard from the board that elected the new president of Union and Planters. Among the twenty directors who met for that purpose on March 11, 1915, only John Pepper could date his service to much before 1900. Most of the others, in outlook as in tenure, were a generation apart from Samuel Read, and to them his go-slow policy had begun to look, said one of them later, "stolid." They had shown Read the deference they felt to be his due for having saved the bank from suspension in 1873 and again in 1878, but now they chose as his successor a man of an altogether different mold. He was Frank Hill.

At the age of forty-one, after a banking career of seven years, Frank Fontaine Hill would accept the bank's highest office with the easy assurance that came naturally to the eldest son and business heir of the South's "merchant prince." Nothing that Napoleon Hill's fortune could command had ever been far from Frank's reach. As a toddler, he had been dressed in frocks designed and handmade by Madame Alexandre. A servant accompanied him when he went off in 1890 to receive a gentleman's education at the University of the South. But after three academically lean years there, he professed great eagerness to make his way in business, and a position had opened up for him at Hill, Fontaine & Company. Four years later the stroke that crippled his father left Frank to assume direction of the family's vast holdings. He was twenty-three at the time.

Over the next seven years, as he moved into the executive posts and board seats vacated by his father, Hill developed a reputation for promoting his various enterprises with the casual exuberance of youth, a quality depicted in a caricature from this period. In it he appears as an auctioneer, jauntily holding the globe high overhead while calling out: "How much am I offered?" The caption reads, "He Sells The Earth."

Parental generosity undoubtedly encouraged his sense of mastery. On his thirtieth birthday, Napoleon and Mary Wood Hill gave him securities and real estate valued, in 1904 dollars, at $336,000. From that point Hill's business and social commitments grew progressively more demanding for the next two decades.

By 1908, when he accepted a vice-presidency at Union and Planters, he was already so absorbed in a swirl of other pursuits that he would have been hard put to serve as much more than a name on the bank's letterhead. Aside from the new banking duties, he headed the Napoleon Hill Cotton Company, sold fire and accident insurance, spent most of each summer at his Cape Cod estate, was a familiar face at the New York Yacht Club and the Chicago Exmoor Country Club, and managed the family's more than one hundred properties, including prime commercial buildings like those occupied by the I. Goldsmith department store and by the Scimitar Publishing Company.

Furthermore, in a partnership with his brother-in-law Samuel Watkins Overton, the father of a future mayor and the grandson of one of the three land speculators who had founded Memphis, Hill dealt in residential real estate. On top of all that, he was developing Mammoth Spring, Arkansas, a 2,205-acre plantation town with gins, mills, houses, and its own hotel, electric power plant, and opera house.

If he had a specialty among these many and varied interests, observers of the day neglected to mention it. But what he enjoyed most, according to a biographical sketch of 1911, was "writing insurance policies and driving about the city in one of his big cars."

He also enjoyed cultivating his image as the richest man in town. A story often told in Memphis at the time has Hill standing outside Union and Planters, smoking an expensive cigar, when an older man who had been regarding him with disapproval, asked: "Friend, how much did that cigar cost?"

"Twenty cents," Hill replied.

"How many do you smoke a day?" the older man asked.

"Oh, six or seven, I suppose."

"Humph!" snorted the man. "Do you realize that if you would save that money, by the time you are as old as I am, you could own that building?" and he pointed toward the bank.

"You don't smoke. Do *you* own that building?" Hill asked, whereupon the man answered no.

"Well," Hill said, smiling, "I do."[1]

The claim was figuratively if not literally true. While never in fact holding title to the bank's main office building, Hill did vote the single largest block of the bank's shares—reportedly large enough to give him working control. In 1914 he had voted those shares as usual to continue Samuel Read in office, even though, like others on the board, he thought the bank was lagging behind the times, and as proof he could point out that its deposits were more than one million dollars behind those of its younger, once smaller competitor, the Bank of Commerce. To friends he confided his desire to "preside in a greater . . . up-to-the-minute" Union and Planters.

That ambition, backed by the shares he voted, proved more than a match for the two old-line bankers who also had sought the presidency after Read's death. Both Vice-president Newton C. Perkins, once president of the State National Bank, and Mississippian J. T. Thomas, president of the Bank of Grenada, had initially rounded up enough votes for the *Press-Scimitar* to report, "U & Ps' Board Split on New President"; but both candidates eventually were persuaded by informal polls of the board to withdraw in favor of Hill.

Having thus emerged as the board's unanimous choice, Hill took office pledging to give Union and Planters "the vigor of young blood, enterprise, aggressiveness and modern ideas." He would start with a clean slate of top executives, for all three senior vice-presidents—Perkins, James Hunter, and John Pepper—waited only a short while before submitting their resignations.

It was not by chance that the new order at Union and Planters arose at the height of the Progressive movement in Memphis. The drive for a "Greater Memphis," well underway since 1903, drew much of its strength from younger, "progress-minded" businessmen who talked of adding the dynamism of an Atlanta to the easygoing Bluff City. Less inclined than their fathers' generation to let municipal growth take its own course, they had pushed for annexation, for the city commission form of government, for more public parks, and more paved streets, of which Memphis in 1905 had twenty-two miles compared to Nashville's two hundred miles. It was this Greater Memphis Movement that supplied not only the theme but also the leading characters in the bank's own program of renewal.

Director Henry Winkelman, of Winkelman Baking Company, had served on the Board of Public Works in 1907 when it finally overcame the resistance of property owners to the front foot assessment, which financed the paving of both Union and Madison on out to Cooper. Frank Hill had run in 1905 with Ed Crump on a reform ticket and won a term on the Board of Public Works, where he introduced the city's first ordinance to control smoke pollution. And two of the other directors were in the thick of a local struggle over what had become the most contentious issue in Tennessee politics: Prohibition.

On one side of the liquor issue was legal counsel Gus T. Fitzhugh, utility and railroad lawyer, unsuccessful candidate for the United States Senate in 1911, and a director of the *Commercial Appeal,* whose editorial page usually reflected his viewpoint. As an "ardent advocate of prohibition," Fitzhugh was a political maverick in a city where the Cotton Exchange, the Businessmen's Club, the City Club, the Merchant's Exchange, and the entire city commission had denounced the legislature's statewide ban on liquor sales in 1909. Even such an outspoken foe of liquor as C. P. J. Mooney, editor of the *Commercial Appeal,* had opposed the law's enactment, on grounds that "prohibition where public sentiment is against it, is a fraud, a deceit, an arrant hypocrisy." But when the law took effect, Mooney joined Fitzhugh in demanding its "strict enforcement."

Mayor Crump, by contrast, was not ready to dismiss public sentiment as lightly as that. Under his administration the city's saloons, said to number between 500 and 1,700 establishments of greater or lesser repute, had continued to operate openly. For that privilege they paid a fine of fifty dollars apiece every Monday and delivered votes to the Crump ticket on election days. Many of the saloons remained in the hands of flamboyant vice lords like Bill Latura, who once telephoned C. P. J. Mooney and threatened to kill the whole editorial staff the next time the paper referred to him as "Wild Bill" Latura. Mooney stopped using Latura's nickname in print, but kept up a blistering yet principled attack on the city hall-saloon alliance.

When Mooney's editorial crusade failed to bring about Crump's defeat at the polls, Fitzhugh and other dry Democrats secured passage of a statute with which to carry the fight beyond the ballot box. Known as the Elkins Act, it granted state courts the power to oust municipal officials who neglected to enforce the prohibition law or the nuisance law against gambling and prostitution. Fitzhugh, in his capacity as a special state prosecutor, filed an ouster suit against Mayor Crump on September 19, 1915. A few weeks later the Chancery Court ordered Crump's removal from office. The reformers rejoiced that they had at last "Put a crimp in Crump," while the ex-mayor's supporters paraded through town with banners defiantly proclaiming "Prosperity for Memphis! Down with the Muckrakers!" and "Hurrah for Crump!"

Driven from office but not from power, Crump still pulled most of the wires at city hall and, having been re-elected to another term prior to the ouster, he planned to resume his official duties early in 1916. But before the start of his new term the Tennessee Supreme Court ruled that the same evidence introduced in the earlier ouster suit could be re-introduced in another one. The case for removal was thus readymade, and Fitzhugh announced that he would file suit the minute Crump assumed office. Uncertain whether to accept that risk, Crump didn't claim the mayor's post when it was legally his on February 12. The delay stretched from one week into the next. Then on the morning of February 22, Crump took the oath of office at nine o'clock, resigned two minutes later, and that afternoon watched the swearing-in of his choice for mayor: Union and Planters' director Thomas C. Ashcroft.

Recruited to the board by Frank Hill, Ashcroft was a new face in local banking and government. He had joined the Associated Press in 1888 and remained there for the next twenty-five years, reporting the Johnstown (Pennsylvania) flood of 1889, covering Bryan's 1896 campaign against McKinley, and later settling in Memphis as editor of the local news bureau. In 1913 Ashcroft somehow managed to step out of the news room and into the presidency of the American Building Loan and Tontine Savings Association; besides the usual functions of a mortgage and savings bank, the American sold a form of tontine insurance, which paid face value and yielded bonus dividends if, and only if, the policyholder lived to a stipulated age. Although outlawed in many states after 1905, tontine plans were legal in Tennessee, and exceptionally profitable to the seller.

Ashcroft had also gone at a gallop from reporting political news to making it. He had held public office, in the State Senate and on the City Commission, for just over a year before becoming mayor of the state's largest city. All the same, he was careful to acknowledge the author of his good fortune. Shortly after taking office he wrote Crump: "I am eternally grateful for the honor you have brought me and the confidence you have reposed in me, and so long as I occupy the mayor's office I shall always consider that you are the real Mayor of Memphis. . . . I am quite desirous of having your photograph in my office. Won't you personally favor me with one?"

When the wish was granted, Ashcroft responded delightedly. "I don't want another day to go by," he wrote, "without expressing to you my sincere thanks and appreciation for the splendid picture you sent me. I certainly did not intend that you should be put to the expense of framing it and am sorry you did so, though, I am frank to say, I could not have selected a more appropriate frame. . . . You have probably noticed that your picture occupies a very prominent place on the wall of my office. Let me assure you that it will be a fixture there so long as I occupy the office."[2]

But even as Crump's likeness peered over Mayor Ashcroft's shoulder, Fitzhugh and the anti-Crump group were breathing down his neck. In July 1916, when they hurled an ouster suit at Vice-mayor W. T. McClain, Ashcroft testified against the vice-mayor. Enraged, Crump stalked into Ashcroft's office and removed the picture from its place of honor.

Such, then, were the experiences in city government that gave Ashcroft, as well as Fitzhugh, Hill, and Winkelman, political instincts of the sort seldom found among Memphis bankers. As public officials they had built constituencies and run election campaigns. As banking officials they would likewise concentrate on winning the public's favor.

The theme of Frank Hill's administration—first, last, and always—was, "he who serves best profits most." Where Samuel Read had locked and bolted the doors to all except tried-and-true customers, Hill chose to be an obliging proprietor who freely extended the hand of welcome. In place of Read's iron law of vigilance, Hill substituted his own patrician "ideal that courtesy must rule in every contact with the public." Considering himself, in the words of one authorized profile, "a gentleman to the manner born," Hill accordingly worked to make "the spirit of *noblesse oblige,* 'rank imposes obligations,' the [bank's] emphatic policy."[3]

He set an example of that spirit by acting at once to better the lot of employees. Dingy work spaces were redecorated and obsolete equipment was replaced in an overall renovation of the bank's quarters during 1915.

Salaries went up by twenty percent, Christmas bonuses were handed out for the first time, and each employee above the level of porter received a life insurance policy compliments of management. The supreme expression of *noblesse oblige,* however, was reserved annually for the eve of Washington's Birthday, when everyone from clerk to vice-president was invited to 1400 Union Avenue for a gala dance at President Hill's Italian Renaissance style mansion, with its huge-columned entranceway flanked by stone lions. Although the setting was hardly designed to put $35-a-week tellers at their ease, Hill encouraged a festive mood. One year the band played on until the last guests were departing at four in the morning.

Hill's graciousness had the desired effect. "It is nothing unusual," observed the *Commercial Appeal,* "for the men and women of this bank to stop work to entertain a friend." Nor was it inconsistent with the bank's new slogan: "Business is friendship." Customers learned that the slogan promised them more than a hearty greeting. Overdrafts, which Read had termed an intolerably "great evil," were now seen as a petty nuisance to be handled with tact and forebearance. No longer did the first-time depositor always have to come recommended by a valued customer before being allowed to open an account. And borrowers could now obtain long-term credit, or accommodation loans. In contrast to the short-term trade loans that moved seasonal inventory from sellers to buyers, the accommodation loan committed banking resources, for periods of one or more years, to the expansion of a company's productive capacity. It furnished working capital, a practice Read had condemned because it made the bank "virtually a partner, dependent for final payment upon the success of the business." Changing circumstances, however, tended to justify management's decision to "broaden the viewpoint" in order "to adequately cope with the requirements of the times." The war that had strangled American trade abroad was beginning to have the opposite effect.

The armies of Europe had marched to war expecting a quick finish. Britain had mobilized, wrote Osbert Sitwell, as if for "a brief armed version of the Olympic Games." Kaiser Wilhelm had told troops heading for the front in August 1914, "You will be home before the leaves have fallen." But after a year of indecisive battles, the armies were mired in trench warfare along a four-hundred-mile line that would hardly vary by so much as ten miles. As their stockpiles ran low, the Allies turned to the United States to buy weapons and supplies in quantity and at any cost. At the same time, neutral countries were calling for food and other products that the belligerents could no longer supply. Recession gave way to boom times as exports to the Allies alone jumped from $825 million in 1914 to $3.814 billion in 1916. There were no more appeals to "bale out the South."

The region's economic prospects improved even more dramatically when the United States entered the war on April 6, Good Friday, 1917. Cotton that year brought twenty-seven cents a pound—the highest price since 1868; and because cotton, unlike other crops, remained free of price controls, its value during the next two years rose like smoke.

Demand also grew for a related product known as linters: these tiny fibers, left on cotton seed after ginning, were essential to the manufacture of gun cotton, explosives, and other munitions. Retail trade picked up across the region as the military sent thousands of recruits south to hastily-erected training camps, one of which, recalled William Alexander Percy, "bulged with five thousand anxious, husky Southerners who believed that if they failed to become officers the war would be lost and they might as well have been born out of wedlock in New England."

Business was further stimulated by President Wilson's program of financing the military build-up not so much through taxation but through borrowing on an unprecedented scale, in five Liberty Loan campaigns. The campaigns came under the direction of Wilson's son-in-law, Treasury Secretary William Gibbs McAdoo, a former resident of Chattanooga, Tennessee. To promote the bonds, McAdoo relied on an ingenious and unremitting publicity blitz such as would not be repeated until the advertising industry came of age in the 1920s. Within less than three years these campaigns raised two-thirds of the money it took to finance the war to a finish and, in the process, gave middle class Americans their first experience of buying on the installment plan and investing in securities. People who had never thought of setting foot inside a brokerage house could now walk into their bank and purchase Liberty Bonds in denominations as small as fifty dollars by making a down payment and agreeing to pay the balance in monthly installments.

McAdoo used his considerable influence to gain the cooperation of bankers and to keep the money supply growing. In June 1917, at his urging, the Federal Reserve Board lowered its reserve requirements, greatly expanding the volume of credit available. The reduction was also intended to win favor among state banks, most of which had declined to join the Federal Reserve on the grounds that its reserve requirements would idle too much of their resources.

In the fall, McAdoo traveled through the South exhorting bankers to join the Federal Reserve System. Arriving in Memphis on October 22, he aroused a "great patriotic outburst" that evening when he spoke from the pulpit of the First Methodist Church. Before leaving town he made at least one important convert, Frank Hill. On the strength of Hill's recommendation, Union and Planters joined the Federal Reserve System toward the end of October 1917. It was said to be the first state bank in Tennessee to do so.

Innovations and firsts of all kinds intrigued Hill. Early in 1918 he started discussing arrangements for opening Union and Planters' first branch. Although most banks still operated only one office, contractions within the banking industry were encouraging the larger institutions to branch out. Smaller banks found it increasingly difficult to survive in Memphis, often because they overextended themselves in competing for business. Of the twenty banks existing in 1912, five had failed or been absorbed, and six others would be gone by 1928. One of them, the Mercantile National, had very nearly been done in by its former president, C. Hunter Raine. Over a period of years Raine had formed the habit of substituting his own checks and due bills for cash and securities belonging to the Mercantile National. When an outside audit revealed these substitutions in 1914, Raine confessed that he had gambled and lost $1.1 million of the bank's funds speculating in cotton futures. That left the Mercantile insolvent, unable to honor the claims of depositors. A group of directors did repay out of their own pockets all account holders who had lost less than one thousand dollars, but hard feelings lingered. Although the Mercantile re-opened with new directors and officers, it had attracted little business. Problems had also arisen with regulators in Washington; the Comptroller of the Currency was criticizing loans to directors and officers amounting to thirty-seven percent of total capital and surplus.[4]

Under the circumstances, selling the Mercantile made sense to its stockholders. Two directors, Jesse Norfleet and Leslie M. Stratton, handled the negotiations with Frank Hill. Norfleet ran the cotton firm of Sledge & Norfleet in partnership with his father, Frank, who had come onto the board of Union and Planters in 1907. Stratton, owner of a wholesale grocery firm and president of the Stratton-Warren Hardware Company, was a friend and neighbor of Hill. Both men would join the board of Union and Planters. The parties needed only eight days to reach an agreement; on February 16, 1918, Union and Planters purchased the Mercantile for the sum of $143,775.

Through the purchase, Union and Planters gained about three million dollars in deposits, increased its authorized capital from 1.5 to 2 million dollars, and converted the Mercantile's banking room into a savings branch. Located at 109 Madison Avenue, the branch was named the Franklin Savings Bank.[5] Within a year the Franklin's books showed twelve thousand active accounts, and the total was increasing at the rate of some ten accounts daily.

By 1919, Hill's program of expansion and modernization had fundamentally changed the character of Union and Planters. Visitors noticed the sleek stylishness, a quality much in evidence during the reception management gave, on September 2, to celebrate the bank's fiftieth anniversary. Potted palm trees and more than two hundred floral arrangements filled the lobby, presenting a sight that reminded one newspaperman more of "a fashionable house adorned for an entertainment than a financial institution." A Hawaiian band played while the officers presented a yellow rose to each arriving guest. "The celebration was unusual," said the *Commercial Appeal,* "and it was the nearest to a society event as any other ever written in the history of the financial world of Memphis."

But more than social polish had been acquired, as anyone who compared the balance sheet of 1919 with the one for 1914 would have seen right away. In a little less than five years, deposits had quadrupled, rising from $5 million to $19.584 million, and resources had ballooned from $7.4 million to $28.427 million. Those figures made Union and Planters not only the leading bank in Memphis but one of the ten largest banks in the South. The rate of growth was nothing short of astonishing. And the economic boom explained only a part of the growth, for scarcely any other bank comparable to Union and Planters had registered so great an increase during the same period. Of all comparable banks in the nation, only five had grown faster than Union and Planters, according to *Financial Age.*

Much of the new business flowed from two sources. One was correspondent accounts. Since 1915 the bank had built up a network of correspondents stretching from West Tennessee into Arkansas and south to Greenville, Mississippi. In Mississippi alone, 145 of the state's 325 banks maintained accounts with Union and Planters. In return for clearing and exchange services, these country banks kept substantial balances on deposit with Union and Planters.[6]

The other, more important, source of new business was the cotton market. Prices were up for the third straight year; at thirty-five cents a pound, the crop of 1919 brought the record-breaking sum of two billion dollars. Pocketbooks bulged in the cotton belt. Even tenant farmers and sharecroppers were said to be "rolling in wealth . . . and engaged in a perfect orgy of money spending." Bullish cotton growers, buyers, and assorted middlemen rushed to expand their operations, and some of them did so on funds borrowed from Union and Planters. Besides the traditional practice of granting loans collateralized by bales of graded, insured, and warehoused cotton, the officers were now lending against the less certain security of land and machinery. These loans—totalling $4.3 million, or nearly twenty percent of all loans—had pumped up assets, at least temporarily. Most of the borrowers owned plantations or compress and storage companies in Memphis or the Delta. Their capacity to repay the notes was only as good as the price of next year's cotton.

Had any one member of the loan committee opposed these credits, they would have been rejected, as the bylaws stipulated. But in those deliberations as in most matters affecting the bank, Frank Hill and the board had come to depend on the judgment of one officer. He was Robert S. Polk. And he was, the *Commercial Appeal* observed, "the dominating figure at Union and Planters Bank and Trust Company."

Bob Polk's many friends described him as a charming, hard-drinking young man full of hustle and push—"a splendid business getter," said a local banker. Orphaned at the age of sixteen, Polk had gone to work as a messenger boy at Union and Planters in 1900. By the time of Samuel Read's death, he had advanced through the ranks to become assistant cashier, answering to Read's second-in-command, Cashier Gilmer Winston. Winston's conservative influence had waned after 1915, as Polk's aggressive, do-anything approach captured President Hill's imagination. Hill had delegated more and more authority to the 36-year-old vice-president, so much that the line between delegating authority and actually sharing it was blurred.

Polk served as president in all but name during the summers that Hill passed at his Cape Cod estate. And it was no secret that the two men had become partners in various business ventures—an automobile dealership, a bakery, a lumber company, a cotton firm—which were financed by Union and Planters. People at the bank had grown accustomed to the idea that, regardless of Bob Polk's title, he was in effect co-president. It was plain to all that Hill trusted him implicitly. As Polk would later say, "Frank Hill has been more than a brother to me."

In the spring of 1920 the economy faltered when wage earners, whose purchasing power had been cut in half by inflation, drastically curbed their spending. Unsold goods piled up in warehouses, factories laid off workers, and prices fell by more than fifty percent over the next two years. Conditions stabilized late in 1921, but agriculture, unlike other sectors, never fully recovered from the depression. Farmers, who had received fifteen percent of national income in 1920, would see their share drop to nine percent by 1929.

Farming costs started climbing after the enactment in 1922 of the Fordney-McCumber Tariff, which raised import duties back to pre-Wilson levels, causing farmers to pay some $426 million more for the supplies they bought. Farmers ended up purchasing goods in a protected market and selling their products in an open world market where prices had fallen more than fifty percent. Land bought in the flush times of 35-cent cotton had to be paid for with the 15-cent cotton of 1920 and the 17-cent cotton of 1921. During those years the majority of Union and Planters' $4.3 million in accommodation loans to planters yielded no more than interest.

Despite the problem with slow loans, management pushed for more growth once the recession ended. In 1922 the bank opened its second branch office, the Main Street Branch, on the corner of Main and Beale. The location was chosen, said Gilmer Winston, in order to do business in "that particular territory which would really be out of touch with our main bank."[7]

That territory was Beale Street, the business and entertainment district patronized by blacks from across the Mid-South. Although Beale Street had its share of fleshpots that never closed, wrote W. C. Handy, "till somebody gets killed," it also was home to mainstream enterprises whose resources exceeded those of many white-operated companies in Memphis. The Mississippi Life Insurance Company, for instance, had raised one hundred thousand dollars in capital and its premium income ran to half a million dollars annually. Robert R. Church, a steamboat cabin boy before the Civil War, had amassed a fortune dealing in Beale Street properties; he left an estate valued at over one million dollars in 1912. And the Solvent Savings Bank, founded by Church in 1906, held deposits of one million dollars, making it the fourth largest black-owned bank in the nation. The color line separating black and white Memphis put Union and Planters' main office "out of touch" with Beale Street, but the branch office there would give the bank a foothold in that promising territory.

Another opportunity to enlarge the branch system was presented by one of the bank's directors, John T. Walsh. Walsh dominated politics in the Irish and Jewish wards of north Memphis. It was said that he "knew every man, woman, and child" there. Most of the men and women kept accounts at the North Memphis Savings Bank, which Walsh had founded in 1904. Located on Main at the northeast corner of Adams, the bank had a loyal following among the neighborhood's businessmen, including Abe Plough, who would turn his small apothecary company into a leading manufacturer of nationally-known products such as St. Joseph's aspirin and Coppertone suntan lotion. But John T. Walsh, at age sixty-nine, was in poor health, and he believed that "a union of interests with the U & P [would] place a greatly enlarged measure of banking services at the command of our customers [while] in no way interfering with the present management." In July, Walsh arranged the sale of North Memphis Savings to Union and Planters for $250,000, payable in Union and Planters' stock.

As Walsh expected, North Memphis' principal officers—Cashier O. H. Hurt and Assistant Cashier Edward Longinotti—continued to transact business without any changes noticeable to most customers. Walsh agreed to serve as a vice-president of Union and Planters, responsible for soliciting accounts from local government. His ability to influence the placement of public funds was considerable, particularly since he had recently patched up his differences with Ed Crump, who would soon open an insurance company in offices above the North Memphis branch.

An accounting firm checked the records, cash, collateral, and securities of Union and Planters in June 1923 and found everything in order. Members of the examining committee thereupon informed their fellow directors that "all loans are in sound and liquid condition." The quality of those assets was a result of "high quality leadership," or so it seemed to the committee members. They concluded that management deserved "unqualified commendation [for its] progressive spirit . . . high degree of skill . . . and sound conservatism." In that they were sadly mistaken.

The extent of their error became front-page news on March 19, 1924 when the *Commercial Appeal* reported that Bob Polk was missing, his whereabouts unknown. Also missing was $41,958 in cash, which had been taken from a teller cage and replaced with due bills endorsed by Polk. The teller said Polk had been making similar substitutions off and on for the past four or five years. An additional $19,284 had been diverted from Liberty Bond accounts and delivered, through a trustee, to Polk.

On March 20, Polk wired Frank Hill from El Paso, Texas: "Will return by next train. Bob." The telegram deepened the sense of mystery. Reporters quizzed Hill about his business partnerships with Polk. The officers fielded calls from agitated businessmen who said that Polk had induced them to borrow and turn over to him money that he claimed they would never have to repay. As rumors spread, Judge J. Ed Richards ordered a grand jury investigation of the shortages, and the directors, meeting on March 22, terminated Polk and voted to issue an additional one million dollars in capital stock. Hill subscribed two-thirds of that amount.

Polk, arriving back in Memphis the same day the board met, assured a small crowd of well-wishers that "everything's all right. There is nothing to worry about, . .   As far as the bank is concerned, there are no problems that can't be solved easily." He declined to answer questions, saying he would have a full statement for the newspapers the next day. No statement came that day.

On Sunday evening Frank Hill and one or two other directors paid a visit to Polk's house, but Mrs. Polk told them that her husband could not see them. Early next morning, a few hours before he was to meet with state bank examiners, Polk put the business end of a loaded thirty-eight caliber revolver to his head and pulled the trigger.

Hill was the only bank official to comment publicly on the suicide. "It's a great shock to me," said Hill. "He came to the bank before I did. Everybody had the utmost confidence in him. If anyone had accused him of being crooked, they would have had me to whip."

At first no one could provide a complete account of the damage done to the bank. Asked to estimate the damage to his own finances, Hill replied: "Certainly, I expect some losses. Nothing that I will not be well able to meet. However, the amount has not been determined yet. There may be no loss at all, but I expect some." Told that talk on the street placed his losses at seven hundred thousand dollars, Hill responded, "That is preposterous," then added, "I certainly hope not."

If anything, the rumored amount was low. Satisfying his obligations to the bank and other creditors would consume what remained of the once immense fortune amassed by Napoleon Hill. By 1935, Frank Hill's net worth had dwindled to ten thousand dollars.

With his credibility as well as his finances in tatters, Hill "retired" from the presidency of Union and Planters. On April 18, the board announced that an agreement had been reached to acquire the Guaranty Bank and Trust Company, and that its president, Frank Hayden, would replace Hill as president of Union and Planters. Hayden, born in Indiana and educated at Harvard, had come to Memphis in 1903 as an appraiser of farm land for a northeastern insurance company. He soon went into business for himself, initially farming on 8,500 acres in the Mississippi Delta and investing in the banks there, and later representing European investors in the farm mortgage market. In 1917 he had organized the Guaranty Bank and Trust, a commercial bank specializing in mortgage lending. It had done well in spite of the treacherous fluctuations in land values. Many businessmen considered Hayden a banker who knew when to be ambitious and when to be cautious. News of his coming to Union and Planters sent the bank's stock from $125 to $132.5, with one block selling for $140 a share.

Essentially, Hayden had accepted a rescue mission. Millions of dollars in assets were imperiled. Outright embezzlements had cost the bank well over $500,000, and the bonding company was resisting the bank's claim for indemnification. Customers claiming to have been defrauded by Polk were pressing the bank to cover their losses. Worse still, a life-threatening percentage of assets was tied up in questionable loans.

Hayden charged off loans of $453,244 shortly after taking office. But even with that purge, loans classified by Hayden as slow or doubtful totaled $8.1 million—or one-third of all loans. Some had been extended to companies controlled by Polk individually or jointly with Frank Hill. Others, about $5 million worth, went to the cotton growers and buyers who had expanded just in time to see cotton prices collapse in 1920. Their notes were so far in arrears that Hayden's only option was to seize through foreclosure the land, mules, and implements pledged, and then to manage the plantations until the day, perhaps years ahead, when the farm lands could be sold at a more or less acceptable price. Everyone connected with the $8 million in loans would suffer. As Hayden said, "a great number of loans on the books have not been a particular help to the borrower, have done the bank no good, and entail considerable credit risk." The question was not whether Union and Planters would lose money, but how much.

CHAPTER 7

The Proposition from Nashville

We were living in a golden age and none
of us thought it would ever end.
—Rogers Caldwell

O N many of the loan files that crossed his desk Frank Hayden penciled instructions to "Push" or "Get Hard" or "Get More Collateral." In some cases, where collection seemed impossible, he directed the bank's counsel to sue delinquent borrowers for title to their memberships in the Memphis Cotton Exchange.

The abrupt crackdown, after years of indulgence, confused and angered many customers, but business was business. With eight million dollars of past due loans and less than one million dollars in surplus and reserves, Hayden was in no position to play the jolly good fellow with delinquent borrowers—or with his associates at Union and Planters. He cut salaries, including his own, by forty percent, and he let the stockholders know that it might be a long while before they saw another dividend check.[1] Profits would have to go toward building up reserves against loan losses.

The stockholders accepted a still larger sacrifice in the fall of 1924. On September 18 they approved the board's proposal to cut the capital stock in two, from $3.75 million to $1.875 million. The 37,500 shares outstanding would be called in and replaced by 18,750 new shares. An investor having, say, $10,000 in stock wound up with $5,000 worth after this form of reverse split. Although the exchange wiped out half the stockholders' equity, it did lessen liability and increase the marketability of the shares.

At their meeting the stockholders also ratified the board's decision to issue an additional 6,250 shares, two-thirds of which were earmarked for new investors. That would bring the total capital to $2.5 million. President Hayden had lined up the necessary subscribers, three of whom joined the board. One was Lant K. Salsbury, president of the world's largest cotton plantation, the British-financed Delta & Pine Land Company at Scott, Mississippi. Another was William Orgill, head of a wholesale hardware house founded in Memphis by his grandfather in 1850. The other new investor-director was R. G. Bruce, whose firm, the E. L. Bruce Company, turned out a substantial amount of the hardwood products that had made Memphis the South's leading manufacturing center for oak flooring, building materials, and crates.

Shortly after the change in capital structure, the officers began preparations for relocating the main office. Hayden, citing the need for larger quarters, had traded the bank's high-rise tower at 81 Madison and given $249,000 for the twelve-story building at 67 Madison, on the corner at Front Street overlooking the Mississippi River. That location would, noted the *Commercial Appeal,* give tenants "the advantage of what breeze there may be stirring."[2]

The building was little more than a year old when Union and Planters opened there on November 29, 1924. Its mortgage bonds had been underwritten in January 1923 by Rogers Caldwell, a Nashville investment banker who had risen from an obscure bond salesman to become the region's preeminent financier, "the Morgan of the South," as he was sometimes called.

A master of creative financing, Caldwell had started out on credit alone, organizing Caldwell and Company in 1917, when he was 27, with $100,000 of capital—which he supplied in the form of his own personal note to the company. Since then he had expanded rapidly, acquiring a commercial bank (the Bank of Tennessee) and an insurance company (Cotton States Life) and underwriting millions in real estate mortgage bonds. If the Caldwell and Company continued to grow by leaps and bounds, quipped a newspaper columnist, "Rogers Caldwell will own everything in ten years." Although Caldwell's operations were confined largely to Nashville in

1924, his ambitions extended across the South; before reaching the age of forty, he would be the most powerful figure in the banking markets of a half dozen cities, including Memphis.

During 1925 and 1926 the problems of asset quality and capital adequacy continued to monopolize the schedules of President Hayden and his executive officers: Vice-presidents Doddridge Nichols, N. Blaine Gentry, Edward C. Tefft, Gilmer Winston, and John J. Heflin, who had managed the Memphis branch of the St. Louis Federal Reserve Bank until accepting a job offer from Hayden. They faced enormous difficulties. Lending capacity was impaired, regulators were calling for substantial improvements in asset quality, and there were more than four hundred slow or doubtful loans on the books.

Through foreclosures, the bank had taken possession of large tracts of cotton lands in Mississippi and Arkansas. Vice-presidents Nichols and Gentry had responsibility for disposing of these plantations, but the demand was weak, and they ended up renting most of the farmland, hoping at least to recover the cost of taxes and upkeep. The word *Planters* in the bank's name was no longer a mere figure of speech; for the next several years the bank would number among its assets a great many horses, mules, turning plows, mowing machines, and boll weevil dusters.

The bank fared better, though, in recovering the losses sustained through embezzlement. In 1926, Gus Fitzhugh won a judgment against the Globe Indemnity Company for the full amount of Bob Polk's bond, $300,000. On top of that, the bank collected $100,000 on the bond of a former vice-president, J. Ramsey Beauchamp. Fitzhugh also defended the bank successfully against at least three suits filed by businessmen claiming to have been defrauded by Polk.

At the same time, profits were returning to healthier levels. Net earnings, which had fallen to $171,929 in 1924, rose to $392,281 in 1925, and then to $438,997 in 1926. Encouraged by that showing, the directors met on January 3, 1927, and declared a six percent dividend, payable semiannually. Commenting on the reinstatement of dividends after a lapse of almost three years, the *Commercial Appeal* editorialized:

> It really is a remarkable tribute to the genius and hard work of Frank Hayden, who took the helm shortly after an embezzlement [and] other irregularities had been discovered. . . . Hayden and his co-workers have converted scandal into success. They deserve the gratitude of the community.

Favorable banking conditions in Memphis had contributed to that success. For the past three years calm had prevailed on the local banking scene, allowing the executives to concentrate fully on internal problems. But the situation took a turn for the worse at the end of 1927. On December 29, Beale Street's Fraternal & Solvent Savings Bank, one of the four largest black-owned banks in the nation, closed down after a three-day run on its deposits. Some 28,000 depositors lost all or part of their savings. Bankers on Madison Avenue dismissed the run as a disturbance confined to Beale Street. Not until six months later did they see that the disturbance on Beale Street marked a shift in the mood of banking customers, white as well as black customers.[3]

Early on the morning of Saturday, July 7, 1928, tellers in the main office began to notice that the lines of customers in front of their windows were growing unusually long. By noon the lobby was jammed with depositors anxious to withdraw their funds. At one point Frank Hayden climbed on top of an officer's desk and assured the crowd that the bank had plenty of cash and would stay open as long as any customer wanted his money. Correspondent banks wired in $2.5 million to Union and Planters' credit at the local branch of the Federal Reserve Bank, which agreed to remain open through the night if necessary.

Hundreds more customers descended on the bank during the afternoon and evening. The officers mingled with them, and Hayden invited them to help themselves to the tub of iced Coca-Colas he had placed in the lobby. Some decided not to close their accounts after all. At nine o'clock, as the crowd thinned out, the bank closed for the day.

"Don't be stampeded by fools and gossips!" urged the *Commercial Appeal* on Sunday. "Five hundred employees of the Commercial Appeal went about their work yesterday with their salary checks from Union and Planters Bank in their pockets. And they will look forward with the usual pleasure to next Saturday, when they will again get checks on the Union and Planters Bank."

But on Monday morning the run started again, and spread to the North Memphis Branch before dying out later in the day. Observers were at a loss to explain what had triggered the run. Its cost, measured in dollar and cents, was fairly low; the net loss in deposits amounted to about one million dollars, or three percent of total deposits, three months afterwards. No less significant were the intangible costs, the erosion in public confidence. Thousands of citizens weren't sure whether their money was safer inside a bank or underneath a mattress. Further evidence of their unease came on

September 26, when the officers of Union and Planters rushed an emergency loan of $300,000 to the Manhattan Savings Bank and Trust Company to stop a run there.

The financial disturbances at Union and Planters and elsewhere probably led Hayden and the board to look at the bank's condition in a different light. The $700,000 in surplus and reserves might see them through normal times, but the times were anything but normal. And if "fools and gossip" alone could stampede depositors, what would happen in the event of an economic downturn or another suspension of dividends? Given the uncertainties, the directors concluded that the bank needed an injection of new capital. The search for a merger partner able to furnish that capital began in August, and three months later Hayden and Directors Fitzhugh and Salsbury had narrowed the choices down to one candidate: Caldwell and Company.

As the talks opened, Rogers Caldwell was near the height of his powers, well on his way to assembling a financial empire of more than fifty interlocking companies worth upwards of five hundred million dollars. He had paid top dollar for his holdings, but their value was rising fast in the Big Bull Market of 1928. U.S. Steel had shot up from $160 to $268 in three months of frenzied trading, and Radio Corporation of America was moving from $85 to $420, even though it had never paid a dividend. When Ford announced the Model A in 1928, half a million people had made down payments without having seen the car and without knowing its price. Real estate and securities commanded unbelievable prices. Economists were predicting that the nation had arrived at a "permanent plateau of prosperity," and their optimism was echoed in the titles of such popular songs as "We're in the Money," and "It Ain't Gonna Rain No More."

Caldwell's stature had grown to almost mythic proportions in the eyes of many Southerners. "Rogers Caldwell is a name to conjure with in the South," wrote a newspaper editor. To a group of young businessmen, he was "the Moses that will lead us out of bondage and make possible for us a new freedom such as the Old South has struggled for since the days of the Confederacy."

In reality, however, Caldwell had expanded almost entirely on borrowed money, backed by the political muscle of his associate, Luke Lea. Lea, a former United States Senator and one-time director of the Atlanta Federal Reserve Bank, tended to make up the rules as he went along. Acting on his own after the Armistice, Lea had led an unsuccessful expedition into Holland to kidnap the Kaiser. Earlier, during two years of maneuvering for influence, he had switched his allegiance from the regular Democrats to the Prohibitionists, then to the Fusionists, and finally sided with the Republicans. More recently he had taken to kiting checks—eventually totaling some ten million dollars—between banks affiliated with Caldwell and Company.

Lea's tactics, said Cordell Hull, were those of a "political gorilla." Despite, or perhaps because of that, Lea was a force to be reckoned with in Tennessee politics. He dictated editorial policy at the three newspapers he owned: the Knoxville *Journal,* the Nashville *Tennesseean,* and the Memphis *Commercial Appeal,* which he had purchased in 1927, working through Gus Fitzhugh. Political hopefuls had to win his favor, or else that of E. H. Crump. And when candidates he had backed were elected, they showed their appreciation by sending lucrative state business to the Caldwell-Lea interests. Governor Henry Horton was especially grateful; he had recently deposited millions in state funds in their banks, fired a highway commissioner who differed with Lea on the awarding of paving contracts, and even built a road through Lea's property to increase its value.

Caldwell and Lea had extended their banking interests to Memphis in May 1928, when they purchased fifty-one percent of the stock in the Manhattan Savings Bank and Trust Company, a strong and profitable bank that had been incorporated in 1885 by Napoleon Hill, among others. Their local go-between in the purchase was William White, president of the City Savings Bank. In July, Caldwell and Lea arranged for the Manhattan to purchase City Savings and to elect White a director and executive vice-president. White then approached Hayden with the idea of combining and recapitalizing the two banks with funds to be raised by Caldwell and Company. When Hayden expressed interest, Caldwell, Lea, Fitzhugh, and Salsbury joined the discussions that led to an agreement on December 27, 1928. The next morning the *Commercial Appeal* reported that the parties had "virtually consumated . . . a gigantic reorganization plan that will give Memphis the largest capitalized bank in the South." Investors, scrambling to buy shares in Union and Planters, drove its price from $160 to $250 in a single day.

The reorganization plan entailed drastic changes. It called for Union and Planters to acquire, through trustees, all the stock of the Manhattan, which would continue to operate as a separate entity with Hayden as president and White as executive vice-president. Union and Planters would then convert to a national bank, while the Manhattan retained its state charter, thereby allowing it to engage in various securities transactions prohibited to national banks. After the conversion, the bank would drop the *and* from its name, becoming the Union Planters National Bank and Trust Company. On the financial side, the capital funds of Union and Planters were to be increased from $3.2 million to $8.37 million, and the Manhattan's by $1.45 million. And $1.7 million of doubtful assets carried by Union and Planters were to be removed and replaced with that amount of cash.

Taken altogether, the plan required $8.32 million in cash. To raise that staggering sum, Rogers Caldwell and Luke Lea, together with Frank Hayden, William White, and Edward Potter, Jr. of the Nashville-based Commerce-Union Bank formed a holding company they called the Bank Securities Corporation. Through it they proposed to raise the $8.32 million by selling stock in the new Union Planters Bank. They planned to convert the 25,000 old shares listed at $100 par into 350,000 new shares at $10 par. Out of that issue, 129,000 shares were to be offered to current stockholders in exchange for their old shares. For those who wanted an immediate profit, Bank Securities promised to buy their shares at $250 apiece. This left 221,000 shares, of which Bank Securities planned to retain 75,000 and market the balance of 146,000 at $63 par. If all went as planned, Bank Securities would clear $870,000 from the stock offering, receive the $1.7 million in doubtful assets, and own enough stock to exercise working control over the new bank.

That, in effect, was the proposition that Hayden placed before the stockholders on January 9, 1929. He began by reminding them that "the problems we have had to meet the past five years have been great, such probably at times to shake your confidence." But those days were over. "We have arrived today," Hayden said, "at a point where every stockholder can get his money back at a profit."

He then explained the proposition in detail. Only one of his listeners, the owner of seventeen shares, voiced an objection. The others seemed intrigued by the deal, particularly once they heard about the potential return on investment. P. H. Norrell, the attorney for Rogers Caldwell brought up the question of dividends, to which Hayden responded: "We have figured that the minimum [profit] would be a million four hundred thousand; and it would take, to pay a 25 percent dividend, $875,000, and I don't think there is any chance in the world of not making that much or more." The proposition carried by a vote of 17 against and 20,577 in favor.

Caldwell and Company, acting for the Bank Securities Corporation, managed to sell most of the 146,000 shares of Union Planters within six

weeks of the stockholders' meeting, but when the date set for reorganization arrived, February 28, the proceeds fell short of the agreed total by
$700,000. To make up the shortage, Caldwell's representative, T. G. Dono-
van, simply handed over deposit slips showing that the necessary funds
had been credited to accounts of Union Planters at the Bank of Tennessee
(Caldwell's chief subsidiary), the Commerce-Union Bank, and the Fourth
and First National Bank, which was controlled by the Caldwell family.
Donovan had no authority to set up deposit accounts at the Commerce-
Union Bank. But Hayden accepted the deposit slips, never suspecting that
they were legally worthless, nor realizing that the Bank of Tennessee did
not have sufficient funds on hand to honor checks drawn on the account.
Without knowing it, Hayden had thus accepted $700,000 in extremely
doubtful assets.

As soon as the transaction was completed, Caldwell and Company began to seek funds from Union Planters. On the very day of the reorganization, Luke Lea saw to it that the bank wired a $500,000 deposit to the Bank
of Tennessee. More deposits followed until, by the end of March, Union
Planters had advanced Caldwell and Company $2.438 million. Fortunately
for the bank, some of its directors noticed that Caldwell was milking the
bank of funds. Their chance to stop the outflow came when the Comptroller of the Currency reviewed the bank's application for a national charter.
They insisted that the Comptroller protect the bank, and as a result the
principals of Bank Securities signed an agreement with the Comptroller to
cease and desist. The letter of agreement, dated April 9, 1929, reads:

Comptroller of the Currency
Washington, D.C.

Dear Sir:

In a meeting held in Memphis, Tennessee, with your examiners,
Wm. R. Young and John S. Wood, the matter of the application of the
Union Planters Bank and Trust Company to convert into a national
bank was discussed at length and in detail. The five undersigned,
Rogers Caldwell, Luke Lea, Edward Potter, Jr., Frank Hayden and
William White, are members of a group that underwrote the reorga-
nization of the Union Planters Bank and Trust Company.

After a full discussion of the matter, the undersigned expressed the
opinion that in view of their large stock interest in the Union Planters
Bank and Trust Company it would be to the interest of the bank that

they would not jointly, nor severally, nor individually, nor any of their corporations, firms, enterprises or underwritings either directly or indirectly, by accommodation loans or otherwise use any of the funds of the proposed Union Planters National Bank and Trust Company or the Manhattan Savings Bank and Trust Company; and it is further provided and agreed that if on the date of the conversion of the Union Planters Bank and Trust Company into a national bank the said Rogers Caldwell, Luke Lea, Edward Potter, Jr., Frank Hayden, or William White, or either of them, jointly or severally, individually, or through any of their corporations, firms, enterprises or underwritings, directly or indirectly owe the Union Planters Bank and Trust Company or the Manhattan Savings Bank and Trust Company, or both, that all the said indebtedness will be paid within six months from the date said Union Planters Bank and Trust Company converts to a national bank.

This agreement on the part of the undersigned is to remain in full force and effect until modified or abrogated by the Comptroller of the Currency.

> Respectfully,
> Rogers Caldwell
> Luke Lea
> Edward Potter, Jr.
> Frank Hayden
> William White

That agreement undoubtedly saved Union Planters. It put the bank's assets beyond Caldwell's grasp, and obligated him to repay the $2.438 million already advanced. The national charter was issued on July 9, thus giving Caldwell until January 9, 1930 to make repayment. The likelihood of that, however, slipped away when the New York Stock Exchange crashed on October 24. Stock prices collapsed as investors unloaded twelve million shares in a market that buyers had all but deserted.

Caldwell, overextended and short of cash, proceeded to milk his subsidiaries dry. From the *Commercial Appeal* alone he obtained $1.128 million. But by December he had only $1.924 million with which to meet demand liabilities of $19.258 million. That same month, Hayden and other directors from Memphis offered to buy a block of the Union and Planters stock held by Caldwell, but he refused. Apparently judging the offer to be an act of insubordination, Caldwell used his controlling interest to remove Hayden from the presidency and replace him with the more pliant William White. White, under pressure from Caldwell, declared an extra "Christmas dividend" of ten percent, despite the rapidly deteriorating economy and the objections of local directors. Whether because of this or for other reasons, Gus Fitzhugh and three other directors resigned from the board. The remaining local directors found themselves increasingly at odds with the group of directors from Nashville, including Rogers Caldwell, his father James and brother Meredith, Edward Potter, Jr., Edwin Warner, and Hillsman Taylor.

As the true condition of Caldwell and Company became better known in 1930, the local directors took a firmer stance against Caldwell. On April 8 the executive committee voted unanimously to withdraw the $700,000 that had been tendered as deposits rather than as cash on the day of reorganization. They also sent Caldwell and Lea a strongly worded letter demanding repayment of the $2.438 million advanced in early 1929. And on July 21 the directors turned President White out of office. In his place they elected Edward P. Peacock, a conservative Mississippi banker with a long and spotless record.

Peacock had helped organize the Bank of Clarksdale in 1900, and during his twenty years as its president had seen it grow into the third largest bank in Mississippi. Asked to comment on Peacock's election, a Memphis banker replied: "Folks in the Delta would put money in Ed Peacock's bank quicker than they would put it into government bonds. UP is gaining a wonderful executive."

Peacock took office during the final days of the House of Caldwell. On November 7, the Bank of Tennessee suspended operations. Its books showed deposits of $10 million—a third of which was state money—but an examination turned up only $32.55 in cash on the premises. On November 14 Caldwell and Company went into receivership. Its collapse set off runs and bank failures in Knoxville and Nashville. From there the panic spread to cities in six other states, where some 120 banks failed, carried down by Caldwell and Company. Of the twenty-one banks once controlled by the "Morgan of the South," only Union Planters remained open for business.

Mr. Alec and the Colonel

Gas	14¢
Caldwell	2¢
Lea	2¢
Horton	1¢
Total	19¢

—Sign expressing a service station
owner's idea of who profited from
Tennessee's five-cent gasoline tax
(November 1930)

A POLITICALLY-CHARGED investigation of Caldwell and Company exposed enough low doings in high places to discredit Tennessee's banking system without, however, leading to any reforms that might have restored public faith in the system. Each new revelation merely fanned resentment and fear. People complained bitterly in late 1930 when word got around that the state would lose most if not all the $6.65 million it had funneled into the Caldwell-Lea banks. Indignant citizens assembled at protest rallies all over the state. There were calls for the impeachment of Governor Henry Horton, and demands that Caldwell and Lea's future role in state roadbuilding be of the "stripe wearing and chain clanging" kind.[1]

Rogers Caldwell was still a name to conjure with, only now the spell worked in reverse. Many people jumped to the conclusion that any business associated in any way with Caldwell was suspect. Those suspicions touched off a minor run at Union Planters on November 5, causing President Peacock to issue a statement that "neither Caldwell and Company nor Rogers Caldwell owe either the Union Planters National Bank or the Manhattan Savings Bank anything whatsoever."

Nine days later, as deposits continued to trickle away, Peacock issued another statement. In it he was again forced by circumstances to be somewhat economical with the truth. Union Planters had severed "all connections with the Caldwell interests of Nashville," he announced, adding that "control and administration . . . are now in the hands of officers and directors who are residents of Memphis." He was telling the truth, if not exactly the whole truth. The Nashville directors had been eliminated from the board. And the Caldwells had recently lost their large chunk of Union Planters stock, but that stock—and the working control that went with it—remained in hands other than those of local investors.

Up until November 11, 1930, Caldwell's Fourth and First National Bank and his Bank Securities Corporation between them owned 145,662 shares, or forty-two percent, of Union Planters. But at the end of business on November 11, runs had cleaned out the Fourth and First National. During meetings arranged that night by the Nashville Clearing House Association, the Fourth and First was absorbed by its chief rival, the American National Bank (later re-named First American).

Among the assets going to American National were 126,000 shares of Union Planters, which Fourth and First had earlier pledged to obtain a $1.8 million loan from American National. That took working control from the Caldwells, for whom American National's president, Paul M. Davis, and its chairman, P. D. Houston, had little use. (Davis would become closely identified with the Crump-McAlister coalition that broke Luke Lea's hold on state politics in 1932).[2]

Although Davis and Houston had no immediate plans to impose their policies on Union Planters, their ownership of thirty-six percent of the bank worried Ed Peacock and the board. It concerned them that working control of Union Planters remained with Nashville bankers, because when banking customers in Memphis thought of Nashville bankers, they tended to think first of Rogers Caldwell.

Peacock's more immediate concern, however, was with the economy, which was headed into the deepest and longest depression in the nation's history. Prices continued to go down in 1931, cotton dropping to six cents a pound. By April 1932, fully one-quarter of all farmland in Mississippi would be in foreclosure, and when Governor Bilbo left office the state treasury contained $1,326.17.

Plummeting real estate values were wrecking the finances of several well-known landowners, including the bank's former president, Frank Hill; in 1933, unable to pay delinquent property taxes of over $30,000, Hill leased his mansion at 1400 Union to a funeral home. Retail sales in Memphis would soon fall to fifty-four percent of their volume in 1929, and bank clearings to fifty-five percent. From the peak of prosperity in August 1929 to the bottom of depression in March 1933, the assets of banks in the South would shrink from $7 billion to $4.7 billion.

The economic contractions had reduced Union Planters business to about what it had been in 1921. A month before the stock market crash the bank carried loans of $25.4 million; two years later, in September 1931, total loans had decreased thirty-nine percent, to $15.5 million. During the same period, deposits fell off twenty percent, from $35.86 million to $28.78 million (in December 1930, six weeks after the failure of Caldwell and Company, deposits had dropped to a low of $22.5 million). Despite the heavy loss of deposit money and earning assets, management turned a profit of about $300,000 and retained $6.16 million in reserves in 1931. With sixty-four cents in cash and reserves for every dollar of deposits, the bank was prepared for hard times.

At the end of eighteen months at Union Planters, Ed Peacock had accomplished all he had set out to do. He had come to the bank intending only to place operations on a sounder footing. Having done that, he left in January 1932, returning full-time to his duties as president of the Bank of Clarksdale. The board elected as his successor Gilmer Winston, who had been with the bank since 1901. He was a careful, meticulous officer and, according to his colleagues, an "invariably gentle" man whose "bearing refuted the . . . supposition that a banker, to be successful, had to be hard-boiled."

Certainly, Winston's credit policies were enlightened, even benevolent, by the standards of the day. He rejected the purely defensive approach, common in 1932, of sitting on assets until better times. "Bankers had begun to hoard," noted Jesse Jones, head of the Reconstruction Finance Corporation. "In the spreading fright," Jones said, "the aim of many bankers was simply to get their institutions in a more and more liquid position, to convert everything possible into cash and let the business of extending credit—the lifeblood of commerce and industry—take shelter until the dark skies cleared."

Winston, by contrast, believed in deploying Union Planters' funds to alleviate the effects of depression locally. In the spring of 1932, when the Memphis school system ran out of money and credit, he permitted the school system to overdraw its account by $450,000. Later on, the bank would honor the "teachers' warrants" that the Shelby County school system issued in order to meet its payroll. The loans not only helped keep the schools open through 1932 and 1933, but also earned the lifelong gratitude of Ed Crump. As an associate of Crump's later explained: "Mr. Crump was always partial to Union Planters because they had honored the warrants one-hundred percent. The other banks wouldn't take them even at a discount."[3] From 1932 until Crump's death in 1954, Union Planters received one-hundred percent of both city and county deposits.

In December of 1932 Gilmer Winston suffered a heart attack that confined him to his bed for the next four weeks. He was still recovering in January 1933 when the nation's banking system began slipping into paralysis. Depositors were beseiging banks in five cities, including the Bank of Commerce in Memphis.

Winston came back to his desk on January 21, the day that the Bank of Commerce lost $500,000 in deposits. The run picked up speed on Monday as depositors withdrew one million dollars. On Tuesday afternoon, with lines of customers extending out the bank's main entrance and for two blocks along Monroe Avenue, the Bank of Commerce closed early. Guards "gently but firmly removed [customers] from the lobby."

Officials of the Reconstruction Finance Corporation (RFC) predicted a city-wide financial panic if the Bank of Commerce failed to open its doors the following morning.[4] They met with President Thomas O. Vinton and major stockholder R. Brinkley Snowden to discuss making a loan that would enable the bank to pay off all its depositors and wind up its affairs. After a hurried appraisal of assets they determined that a bailout would require $13 million. The RFC agreed to lend $12.5 million, provided that Vinton and Snowden convinced other local bankers to lend the balance of $500,000. It was the RFC's policy to require local participation; without it, the loan would not be granted.

Obtaining commitments for half a million dollars proved none too easy for Vinton and Snowden; apparently only one of their fellow banking executives was willing to consider such a loan: around midnight Gilmer Winston joined the meetings underway at the Bank of Commerce.

Winston leaned toward granting the loan, but first he wanted the concurrence of the Nashville interests represented by Paul Davis of the American National Bank. Someone then saw to it that both Jesse Jones and United States Senator Kenneth D. McKellar telephoned Davis, explaining the gravity of the situation and, in McKellar's words, "insist[ing] upon Davis arranging this loan."[5] Along about one o'clock Davis gave Winston the go-ahead, and Union Planters put up the $500,000.

Tensions eased when the Bank of Commerce opened an hour ahead of time, ready to pay off depositors. Its assets were eventually liquidated for the benefit of creditors. Later in 1933 some of its former stockholders, with financial support from the RFC, organized a new bank, which they named the National Bank of Commerce.

As calm returned to Memphis, panic rose to unmanageable proportions elsewhere. On February 4, Huey Long shut down all Louisiana's banks in order to save the faltering Hibernia Bank and Trust in New Orleans. Ten days later Governor Comstock ordered an eight-day banking "holiday" in Michigan, where talks had broken down between Henry Ford and the RFC on ways to shore up Detroit's banks. While re-openings were being delayed in Louisiana and Michigan, Indiana declared a holiday on February 23; Maryland followed on the twenty-fifth, Arkansas on the twenty-seventh, Ohio and Kentucky on the twenty-eighth. Commercial depositors in those states immediately started drawing down their balances in other states where banks were still operating. To reduce the outflow of funds, California, Pennsylvania, Mississippi, Oklahoma, New Jersey, and Tennessee froze their banks' deposits in whole or in part. As of March 1, withdrawals in Memphis were limited to one hundred dollars, or ten percent of balances up to five thousand dollars and an additional five percent of any balance over five thousand dollars.

By Saturday, March 3, 1933, there were 5,504 banks in thirty-one states on holiday, their deposits of $3.43 billion dollars beyond the reach of depositors. Then, at 12:30 on the morning of March 4, a few hours before Franklin Roosevelt was to be sworn in as President, Illinois and New York suspended banking. That, said Jesse Jones, "was the knockout blow." Upon hearing of the closings in New York and Illinois, President Hoover remarked: "We are at the end of our string. There is nothing more we can do."

Two days after his inauguration, President Roosevelt announced a week-long banking moratorium during which no bank could "pay out, export, earmark, or permit withdrawals or transfers . . . of gold or silver coin or bullion or currency." Until examined and judged solvent, banks were allowed only to make change, cash checks drawn on the Treasurer of the United States, create special trust accounts for new deposits, and permit access to safe-deposit boxes. Federal or state examiners would determine the condition of all banks, dividing them into three classifications: Class A banks, with capital intact; Class B banks, with impaired capital but sufficient assets to pay off depositors; and Class C banks, with assets insufficient to satisfy all depositors. Only the Class A banks would be allowed to re-open on March 13.

The examiners arrived at Union Planters on Saturday, March 11, and completed their work the same day. Their report was favorable, for the most part: the bank would receive a Class A rating. But the examiners, judging the assets of the affiliated Manhattan Savings Bank to be deficient by $1.232 million, planned to give it a Class C rating.

Adverse publicity would result if the Manhattan failed to re-open, the directors concluded. Meeting in special session at nine o'clock, they voted to assume the deposit liabilities of the Manhattan and charge off the $1.232 million against profit and loss at Union Planters. Stock in the Manhattan would continue to be held in a trust for the stockholders of Union Planters, thereby allowing the board of Union Planters to carry on certain arm's length transactions with the trustees of the Manhattan holding company. Albert Wooldridge was named executive vice-president of the Manhattan, which reopened on March 13 as a branch of Union Planters.

Another issue raised by the bank examiners involved President Winston's health: could he, they asked, serve effectively while recovering from a heart attack? The question also seems to have occurred to Paul Davis. Just before the moratorium Davis had sent Union Planters his third-ranking officer, Vance J. Alexander. A tall, powerfully-built man with an incisive mind and a charming manner, Alexander had grown up in the small coal-mining town of Jasper, Tennessee, graduated from Vanderbilt University in 1906, then worked at two country banks before joining American National in 1920. His subordinates called him "Mr. Alec," and his superiors thought highly of him. Said P. D. Houston, American's chairman: "Vance possesses a rare ability to fully comprehend problems . . . reach decisions without undue delay . . . [and] he can break bad news in such a way as to retain anyone's friendship."

Besides assigning Alexander to the bank, Paul Davis asked a local attorney, Colonel J. Walter Canada, to look over the bank's situation. The choice of Colonel Canada was not surprising, since he had served for the past three years on the board of the *Commercial-Appeal,* working to reconcile differences between a group of local stockholders and another group in Nashville. Canada had built a thriving practice, largely by representing railroads such as the Missouri Pacific, the St. Louis-Southwestern, and the Frisco System. Small and compact of frame, Canada carried himself like a military man, which he had been during the Spanish American War; he had learned to pilot an airplane at the age of fifty.

Colonel Canada and Vance Alexander hit it off right away. They both saw much room for improvement at Union Planters. Davis apparently felt the same way; he reportedly was displeased that the bank had deferred its dividend in spite of having a large surplus. In fact, Davis had been urging the directors to reduce the bank's size by closing the Manhattan and the North Memphis branches and paying out in dividends a large portion of the surplus.[6]

But an altogether different plan started unfolding the first week of April, when Union Planters became not only a professional but also a business interest for Colonel Canada. With Davis' backing, Canada recruited allies among local businessmen and, during called meetings of the stockholders and directors on April 8, brought about a reorganization so thorough that the *Press-Scimitar* reported: "Canada's Group Heads Union Planters Bank." The stockholders voted twelve directors off the board.[7] Eight new directors were elected: Canada, Vance Alexander; lumberman Robert M. Carrier; Richard M. Dozier, Memphis agent for the Missouri Pacific; tractor dealer F. O. Halloran; R. O. Johnston, president of the Commercial & Industrial Bank; William L. Loeb, of Loeb's Laundry; and Edward P. Russell, of Canada's firm. The reconstituted board then met, elected Vance Alexander president, appointed Canada general counsel, and named Gilmer Winston to the newly-created post of board chairman.

The reorganization plan had developed quickly, perhaps in less than a week's time. It "came about rather suddenly," Alexander confided to a friend. "I was only given a few days in which to make up my mind," he wrote. "In fact, when I first came here I did not come with the intention of staying. . . . You can imagine what turmoil I have been in."

But Vance Alexander had a knack for landing on his feet. For an outsider, and a Nashvillean at that, he showed remarkable sensitivity to the ways of Memphis. Frank Hayden, now in the mortgage lending business, was one of the first to compliment him on his progress. "As a 'fureigner,' " wrote Hayden on April 21, "you are making rapid strides. A great many people have come to me and repeated most favorable comments about you. The bank has faltered considerably in the last year and I think you have a wonderful opportunity to re-establish it and I am sure you will do so."

Vance Alexander inherited several problems requiring prompt attention. One was the $1.2 million loss the bank had sustained when it absorbed the Manhattan Savings Bank. Upon going over the transaction, Alexander and Colonel Canada determined that the terms could be modified so as to recapture the charge off. Canada accordingly re-drew the agreement and, in meetings that Senator McKellar set up with the Comptroller of the Currency, won permission to restore the $1.2 million to capital assets by taking a note for that amount from the trustees of the Manhattan holding company.

Another problem, and one not so speedily resolved, grew out of the loan to the Bank of Commerce. The terms of the loan had not been reduced to writing; officials of both banks, under pressure, had simply arrived at a verbal agreement. But the next day their recollections of the agreement differed markedly. Gilmer Winston thought that the Bank of Commerce had pledged the "cream of its assets": $500,000 in cash and $1.5 million in guaranties of the directors. President Vinton maintained that no specific assets had been assigned. To make matters worse, national bank examiners were now criticizing the loan.

Alexander wrote Vinton on April 19, demanding payment on maturity in July. "One of the first matters of importance that has come to my attention," he wrote, "is the matter of the $500,000 loan that was made available to your bank to prevent a disaster to you and your directors as well as the entire community. . . . This loan has brought considerable criticism of the Board of Directors and the continuation of it unpaid will result in criticism of myself."

When the loan went unpaid, Alexander repeatedly asked the RFC to take it up. In one letter to an RFC official, he argued that the note jeopardized the bank's standing with customers and investors. "The general public in Memphis," he claimed, "have an impression that this loan is an obligation that probably the Union Planters National Bank will have to take a considerable loss on. . . . One of the reasons that I have been unable to interest Memphis capital in the purchase of the Nashville stock is the uncertainty of the final outcome."

Alexander eventually took his case all the way to Jesse Jones, to no avail. "We all argued with [Jones]," Alexander wrote Senator McKellar, "but he seemed to want to continue the liquidation of the assets and make payments from time to time rather than take the whole obligation up. He told me he wanted to keep us in the picture. For what reason I do not know. . . . In a joking manner he offered me $250,000 for our debt. I told him that if he offered $250,000, knowing him as I did, I knew the debt was worth par, $500,000." Alexander did, however, stop the old Bank of Commerce from converting $2 million of assets into stock of the First National Bank; and he continued to assert the bank's claim until large chunks of principal began to be repaid in 1935.

By the end of 1933, Alexander had results to show the stockholders: profits of $421,671 and a three-percent dividend. In 1934 Alexander pushed hard for new deposits; he and the bank's new business officer,

O. K. "Mike" Earp, obtained sizable accounts from General Motors, the American Tobacco Company, and American Airways, while Colonel Canada secured deposits from the treasurers of four railroads he represented. Moreover, correspondent bank balances, which had amounted to $3.1 million in 1932, rose to $9.5 million—the highest mark since 1919. Those gains pushed total deposits to $40.6 million, or about $5 million more than the peak level attained in 1929. The increase represented sound growth, a solid base from which the Alexander administration would build year by year, taking deposits to $70.1 million by 1939.

Lending also revived in 1934, though outstanding loans would remain below pre-depression levels until 1938. The adoption in 1934 of federal deposit insurance undoubtedly stimulated lending activity. By covering balances up to $5,000, the insurance program virtually eliminated the threat of runs and effectively freed up funds that might otherwise have been consigned to reserves. After the coverage went into effect at Union Planters, management reduced surplus and reserves from $9.8 million to $3.1 million. Outstanding loans, which had been stuck at about $13 million through 1932 and 1933, jumped to $23.9 million during 1934.

Alexander committed nearly one million dollars to mortgage loans backed by the Federal Housing Administration, which gave many wage earners their first chance at home ownership. A still larger portion of funds went into the cotton market, where the bank had lost heavily ten years ago. This time, however, the lending took place under the watchful eye of an expert, Director Lytle McKee, a past president of the Memphis Cotton Exchange and partner in the cotton firm of Sternberger-McKee. Under his direction the bank began to participate in the price support loans granted by the Commodity Credit Corporation, which pegged cotton at twelve cents a pound in 1934. McKee also found buyers who paid $548,000 for most of the bank's remaining farmlands.

As business picked up, Alexander and his closest associates on the executive committee, Colonel Canada, Lytle McKee, and Bob Carrier, gradually regained control of the Union Planters stock held in Nashville. In August 1934, local trustees acquired 30,000 shares that Fourth and First Banks, Inc. had pledged on a loan from Manhattan Savings. The following year Lytle McKee, as agent, bought 10,000 shares from the Commerce-Union Bank. Finally, on June 29, 1936, local trustees bought 39,536 shares from the American National Bank in Nashville. That purchase, Alexander told the press, "puts control of the stock of the bank in the hands of Memphis—where it belongs."

William M. Farrington was the chief organizer of Union and Planters and its president from 1869 to 1874.

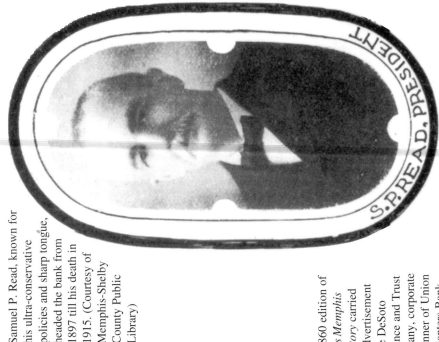

Samuel P. Read, known for his ultra-conservative policies and sharp tongue, headed the bank from 1897 till his death in 1915. (Courtesy of Memphis-Shelby County Public Library)

The 1860 edition of *Long's Memphis Directory* carried this advertisement for the DeSoto Insurance and Trust Company, corporate forerunner of Union and Planters Bank.

HOISTING THE STARS AND STRIPES OVER THE POST-OFFICE AT MEMPHIS, TENNESSEE.—SKETCHED BY MR. ALEXANDER SIMPLOT.—[SEE PAGE 423.]

The federal occupation of Memphis, after a brief, one-sided battle on June 6, 1862, opened the way for several of the bank's organizers to amass large profits in trading between enemy lines.

Interior Union and Planters Bank

Union and Planters Bank Bldg.

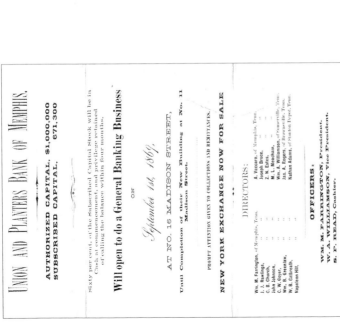

A handbill distributed in August 1869 claimed that Union and Planters would open with subscribed capital of $671,300, or roughly four times the capitalization of Memphis' largest bank, the German National. "This institution will be of the greatest possible benefit to our city," predicted the *Memphis Daily-Appeal*, "and is demanded by the business community."

From 1870 to 1906, the bank operated out of a three-story brownstone at 11 Madison (now 73 Madison). In 1924 the main office was moved back to this city block at Front and Madison, and it would remain there into the early 1990s. (Courtesy of Memphis-Shelby County Public Library)

Napoleon Hill, the "merchant prince of the South," owned the largest cotton and supply house in the nation when he was elected president of the bank in 1885. (Courtesy of Southern Historical Collection, University of North Carolina at Chapel Hill)

Charles Wesley Goyer, the bank's president from 1874 to 1881, had worked his way from trading with flatboatmen in the 1840s to running Memphis' leading wholesale grocery house, C. W. Goyer & Company. (Courtesy of Memphis-Shelby County Public Library)

James Adolphus Omberg was the bank's first (and sole) teller, in 1869; he resigned in 1879 to become cashier of the Bank of Commerce, and in 1907 was elected president of the First National Bank.

Director John Johnson was an Irish immigrant who had started in business as an Indian trader along the St. Francis River in Arkansas. Elected mayor of Memphis in 1869, Johnson took office only to find "the city without a dollar of cash in her treasury."

Jefferson Davis banked at Union and Planters during his years in Memphis. This check, dated "Sept 72," is made out to his wife, Varina.

The yellow fever epidemic of 1878 almost turned Memphis into a ghost town. "The death rate is over one hundred every day," wrote a city policeman in September. "The undertakers can't bury them fast enough. We find a lot that have been dead three or four days. My God it is fearful." (Courtesy of Memphis-Shelby County Public Library)

Dressed in Gilded Age finery, Mr. and Mrs. Napoleon Hill pose for
the camera in a *trompe l'oeil* setting fit for Greek gods and
goddesses. (Courtesy of Southern Historical Collection, University of
North Carolina at Chapel Hill)

"Cotton, cotton, cotton . . . the color of the bluffs and the color of the new cotton bales
piled along the slope were almost precisely the same. . . . the irregularly broken
brownness of the bluffs themselves helped out the fancy that Memphis was actually
built on cotton. Allegorically speaking, that is strictly true."—Lafcadio Hearn, 1877
(Courtesy of Memphis-Shelby County Public Library)

690th Meeting

Present

Napoleon Hill
James H. McDavitt
J. N. Snowden
Wm. A. Williamson
Benj. Babb
J. P. Read.

Union & Planters Bank of Memphis

Tuesday December 6th. 1887

A Special Meeting of the Board was held this day Mr. Napoleon Hill, presiding.

Mr. Hill explained that on yesterday the Governor and Comptroller of Tennessee, and a representative of the State Treasurer had a Conference with the Bank Officers of Memphis, at which it was asked that the Banks of this City should lend the State of Tennessee $200,000. to enable the State to promptly pay Coupon interest due January 1st.

The State Officers proposed to execute notes to each Bank, according to the respective amounts prorated to each, dated December 15. 1887 and would pay them in 60 days, and would allow the money to remain in the Banks, until wanted for paying the Coupons.

The Banks unanimously agreed to respond, subject to the approval of their respective Boards, and $30,000 was agreed upon as the apportionment of this Bank.

Mr. Hill stated that this Directors Meeting had been called to consider the propriety of making the aforesaid loan.

After discussing the matter quite fully.

Upon motion of Mr. Williamson, seconded by Mr. Snowder it was unanimously resolved that this Bank should make the loan of $30,000 to the State of Tennessee.

No further business appearing on motion the Board adjourned.

J. P. Read Ass.

Napoleon Hill
Pres.

The board minutes of December 6, 1887, record one of several instances when Union and Planters helped the State of Tennessee meet its financial obligations.

Cotton factor Allison C. Treadwell served as the bank's president from 1881 to 1885.

Bankers' Row on Madison Street in 1895: Union and Planters' office was just across the alley in the right foreground. Half a block to the north was the saloon-lined alleyway known as Whiskey Chute, which was later given the more staid name of Park Lane. (Courtesy of Memphis-Shelby County Public Library)

Memphis, Tenn.,

Jan. 4th, 1892.

To the President & Directors

of the

Union & Planters Bank, Memphis.

Gents:-

We, your Special Committee, appointed to make the usual semi-annual examination of the assets and condition of the Bank
generally, beg to report that we performed our duty at the close
of business, Thursday 31st Dec. Every piece of paper held by the
Bank, with the collaterals attached thereto was carefully examined
and we regard it all as secure and satisfactory except the following, which we think worthless and recommend charging same to Profit
& Loss account.

    W. W. Butler ----------$ 250.00;

    J. S. Cross ------------ 488.05;

    H. B. McCaully ------------ 52.16;
                                _____
    Total ------- --$

The cash was counted and found to be $ 100 86/100 over the re-
quired amount. We found the net profits for past six months to be
$ 3//2/5, which we think an excellent showing considering the
general condition of the country.

            Respectfully submitted. J R Pepper
                                    J H McDavitt
                                    Chas N Grosvenor

Bank examinations in the 1890s were usually completed internally with a minimum of fuss
and paperwork. This one-page report of Union and Planters' condition in January 1892 is
signed by Directors J. R. Pepper, J. H. McDavitt, and Charles N. Grosvenor.

Union and Planters' Bank

S.P.READ, PRESIDENT

1903

J.D.McDOWELL
ASSISTANT CASHIER

JNO.R.PEPPER
VICE PRESIDENT

The teller cages inside Union and Planters stand out like medieval battlements in this turn-of-the-century view.

From 1906 till 1924, Union and Planters' main banking room was located on the ground floor in one of Memphis' first "skyscrapers," the Tennessee Trust building at 77 Madison (now 81 Madison).

President Samuel P. Read, in 1914, was the oldest banker still active in Memphis, and probably one of the few octogenarians running a sizeable bank anywhere else in the nation.

President Frank F. Hill considered himself "a gentleman to the manner born," and accordingly worked to make "the spirit of *noblesse oblige,* 'rank imposes obligations,' the [bank's] emphatic policy" from 1915 till 1924.

A gathering of the board in 1919. From left to right: unidentified, H. T. Winkelman, Robert Polk, Jesse Norfleet, unidentified, Harry Cohn, Noland Fontaine, Frank Hill, Gilmer Winston, John McDowell, unidentified, Guston Fitzhugh, unidentified, Leslie Stratton, unidentified.

In the 1920s, Edward Hull Crump, who was said to have "run Memphis like a rural plantation," opened an insurance company in offices above the bank's North Memphis branch.

Clerks at the North Memphis branch gathered for this photograph in 1923.
(Courtesy of J. W. Pinner)

Cotton was King in Memphis and his throne was on Front Street, pictured here at the turn of the century.
(Courtesy of Memphis-Shelby County Public Library)

Frank Hayden accepted the presidency of Union and Planters in 1924, at a time when the bank was in deep trouble.

In 1922 the bank opened a branch office on the corner of Main and Beale, at the edge of a business and entertainment district patronized by blacks from across the Mid-South. (Courtesy of Memphis-Shelby County Public Library)

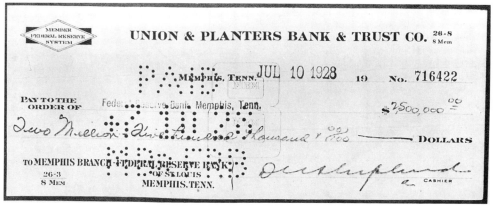

In 1928, management returned $2.5 million that correspondent banks had wired in to see Union and Planters through a run on its deposits.

Stacy _____ PLANTATION 3/22/193 2

Memphis Office:

Gentlemen—

I regret to report the death of Mule No. _____

named *Dag* _____ age _____

on _____ *Stacy* Plantation

Inventory Value $ _____

Caused by _____

Remarks:

Yours truly,
J. W. _____
Manager

Because of bad cotton loans made in the early 1920s, the bank wound up owning and managing many thousand acres of cotton lands, including the Stacy Plantation, whose overseer here advises the bank of the death of a mule named "Dag."

Rogers Clark Caldwell gained working control of Union and Planters in 1929, only a few months before his financial empire began to crumble. (Courtesy of Chattanooga Public Library)

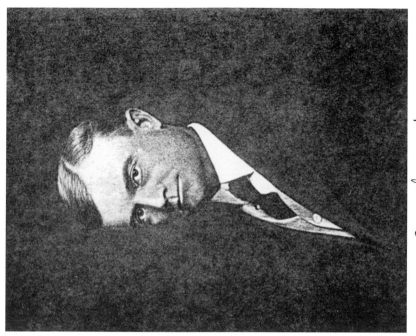

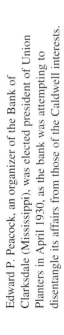

Colonel J. Walter Canada orchestrated a far-reaching reorganization of management and the board in 1932.

Edward P. Peacock, an organizer of the Bank of Clarksdale (Mississippi), was elected president of Union Planters in April 1930, as the bank was attempting to disentangle its affairs from those of the Caldwell interests.

President Vance J. Alexander, "Mr. Alec," led the bank during its longest period of sustained growth, from 1932 until his semi-retirement in 1958.

United States Senate

COMMITTEE ON
POST OFFICES AND POST ROADS

April 17, 1933

Hon. V. J. Alexander,
Union Planters Bank and Trust Co.
Memphis, Tennessee.

My dear Mr. Alexander:

Further answering your letter, I want to congratulate
Memphis on having obtained you as a citizen, and to say
that I know the Union Planters Bank will be splendidly run
by you. I had intended to write you before but you happen
to know something about the mail situation in my office and
I hope you will escuse me.

The Union Planters Bank was started in 1869. For a long
time Mr. Napoleon Hill of Memphis was its President, and
after that Mr. S. P. Read was its President. I was the
Attorney in the Bank in those days and for a number of years
before I first went to Congress. It is a splendid institution.
It is one of the finest institutions we have in the State. It
has done a wonderful work in Memphis and I am sure under your
wise leadership it will continue to hold the high place that it
has held in the banking, business, manufacturing and mercantile
world in Memphis.

With kindest regards and warmly congratulating you, I am

Sincerely your friend,

Kenneth McKellar

Vance Alexander and Senator Kenneth McKellar often consulted each other on matters such
as federal patronage in West Tennessee, banking legislation before the Congress, and Union
Planters' dealings with regulatory agencies. In this letter, McKellar gives a capsule history of
the bank.

The bank's main office building was raised to nine stories on Front and extended down Madison to Center Lane in 1952. On the ninth floor, overlooking the Mississippi, management opened a private dining room that would welcome thousands of the bank's customers over the years, as well as a host of celebrities, including Pablo Picasso, Winthrop Rockefeller, Danny Thomas, Norman Vincent Peale, and Cybill Shepherd.

The main banking room of Union Planters, as it looked in 1952.

Vance Alexander examines a $545 Farmall tractor displayed in the bank's lobby. The sign in the background says that the bank will be closed on July 14, in observance of the birthday of General Nathan Bedford Forrest.

Vance Alexander maintained cordial relations with Ed Crump, pictured here in 1948. Union Planters received one hundred percent of city and county government deposits until Crump's death in 1954.

E.H. CRUMP & CO.

INVESTMENT BANKERS

REAL ESTATE LOANS-MORTGAGE BONDS
INSURANCE-REAL ESTATE

110 ADAMS AVENUE

MEMPHIS, TENN.

3
TO
25
YEAR
EASY PAYMENT
REAL ESTATE
LOANS

MORTGAGE LOAN CORRESPONDENT
METROPOLITAN LIFE INSURANCE CO.

Oct. 5, 1953

Mr. Vance Alexander,
Union Planters National Bank
Mr. Aaron Scharff,
Lowenstein's,
Memphis, Tennessee.

Dear Friends:-

    Doubtless you read the feature "Back Drop" in last Sunday's Commercial Appeal in which Bob Gray said in part :

    "Then something happened. Maybe E.H. Crump, Shelby County political leader, became disgruntled with such individuals as Vance Alexander of the Union Planters National Bank and Aaron Scharff of Lowenstein's who stood to gain business-wise from the location of a Front and Monroe garage location."

    That statement was manufactured from whole cloth and absolutely destitute of any semblance of truth. I never made a statement of that kind to any one or even thought it. I always said that if the city constructed anything at the Front and Monroe location, it should be built in a business-like way on a business basis that contemplated the venture eventually paying off the investment -- just as Union Planters and Lowenstein's have always done so successfully. Mildly expressed, Bob Gray's statement was very, very far from the truth.

    With high personal regards and best wishes to you both,

I am,

Very sincerely,

EHC:H

The South's Largest Insurance Agency

Critical news stories were sure to draw a rebuttal from Crump ranging from the vitriolic, name-calling variety to this more temperately worded letter of explanation to Vance Alexander.

Serving every nook and cranny of Greater Memphis with eleven well situated Offices affords an incomparable Financial Service to our patrons.

By 1952 Union Planters operated ten branches, or approximately twice the number of its largest competitor.

John E. Brown (right) served as chief executive from 1963 to 1967, when he was succeeded by C. Bennett "Ben" Harrison (left).

William M. Matthews, Jr., "brilliant, intimidating, hard-driving, a creative genius," headed the bank from 1974 till 1984.

J. Armistead "Army" Smith joined
Union Planters as head of commercial
and retail operations in 1985, became
vice-chairman of Union Planters
Corporation in 1989, and was
president of Union Planters National
Bank from 1989 to 1992.

Kenneth W. Plunk, president of
Union Planters Bank, 1992–

Jackson W. Moore was elected
president of Union Planters
Corporation in 1989.

Benjamin W. Rawlins, Jr., chief executive officer of Union Planters Corporation,
1984–   (Courtesy of Frank Braden Photography)

"Sane, Conservative Openings"

*You have done a marvellous job since you
took over a fine old rundown institution
and made it into the great bank it is today.*
—J. C. Bradford to Vance Alexander (1952)

THE Great Depression became history when the United States went to war in December 1941. Over the next five years, as Washington invested more than seven billion dollars in Southern military bases and war plants, the South entered a period of robust growth. During those years the region's per capita income rose 120 percent above the level of 1939.

In Memphis, the defense industry became a major employer for the duration of the war, pumping large payrolls into the economy and attracting some 40,000 workers from surrounding areas. By decade's end, Memphis's population would increase by roughly a third, going to 396,000.

The economic resurgence presented new opportunities for Union Planters, and President Alexander was quick to capitalize on them. Management soon opened a strategically placed branch office eighteen miles north of Memphis, in Millington, near DuPont's sprawling Chickasaw Ordnance Works and close to a Naval air station, training center and hospital. Lending activity ranged even farther from Memphis; during 1942 the bank financed construction projects at military bases in Mississippi, Florida, and Alabama.

Always on the lookout for what he called "sane, conservative openings,"

Alexander laid stress on developing a highly efficient system of gathering deposits, which represented a low-cost source of funds, since the money could be taken in at no interest expense (or 1.5 percent on time deposits) and then lent out at rates of from three to six percent.

As one means of attracting deposits, Alexander established a system of branch offices within easy reach of citizens in outlying districts. Customers could thus transact business without driving into downtown Memphis—no small advantage at a time of gasoline and rubber rationing. Responsibility for opening the initial series of branches was given to Executive vice-president Doddridge Nichols. The first of them, the Cleveland Street Branch, opened in June 1941 at 270 North Cleveland, a short walk from Sears, Roebuck's distribution center off North Parkway. Two others followed in 1945: Southside, at 284 East McLemore, and Highland Heights, at 3337 Sumner.

By the end of the 1940s Union Planters would be operating eight branches, or twice the number of its closest competitor, the First National.

An equally important source of deposit money and new business was the correspondent department, which functioned as a clearinghouse and central bank to hundreds of the region's small-town bankers, participating in their over-line loans, entertaining them when they came to Memphis, furnishing credit information and advice on securities trading, and even supplying them with hard-to-find tickets to football and baseball games in distant cities.

That network of correspondents had been expanded many fold by Alexander's second-in-command, Executive Vice-president Isaac H. "Ike" Wilson. A one-time errand boy for a country bank in West Tennessee, Wilson had moved to Memphis as a state banking examiner before accepting an executive position at the Manhattan Savings, in 1930. He had gone on the board of Union Planters three years later and, after the death of Gilmer Winston in 1939, Wilson officially took charge of commercial lending and assumed the duties of chief operating officer. He was considered a strong chief-of-staff to Vance Alexander. As one vice-president later recalled, "Mr. Alec knew how to bring in the business and Ike Wilson knew how to handle it."[1]

Among country bankers Wilson was an able business getter in his own right. Working with vice-presidents Elbert Land and H. E. Roberts, he had brought correspondent business to the fore; between 1934 and 1941 correspondent balances at Union Planters had risen from $3.1 million to $37.4 million. The bulk of those deposits came from 103 banks in Mississippi,

82 banks in West Tennessee, and another 47 in Arkansas. Among the larger ones were the First National Bank of Blytheville, Arkansas; the Grenada National Bank of Grenada, Mississippi; the First National Bank of Jackson, Tennessee; and the Bank of Clarksdale, still headed by Union Planters' old friend and former president, Ed Peacock. Taken altogether, the balances of these banks sometimes accounted for as much as thirty percent of the bank's total deposits, and seldom for less than fifteen percent of the total.

Although loan growth remained sluggish through the war years of rationing and the freeze on non-essential construction, Alexander and Wilson were able to deploy funds more effectively after V-J Day in 1945. By then, consumer demand had reached seismic proportions. Bottled up first by the Depression and then by rationing, consumer spending broke loose once people were again able to buy the cars, appliances, new houses, and other things they had been denied. In 1947 alone, Union Planters committed $2 million to FHA-insured loans for the construction of apartment buildings in Memphis, Chattanooga, Knoxville, and Louisville.

The bank also stepped up installment lending, which Vice-president Edward Longinotti had started on a modest scale back in 1927, when that form of lending had yet to catch on with many Southern bankers. In 1946, Alexander told the stockholders of his plan to "finance installment purchases of consumer durables on a national scale," and that year Longinotti's department began to buy car loans produced by local auto dealers, by General Motors Acceptance, and Ford Credit, as well as millions of dollars of consumer installment loans originated by Sears, Roebuck and Company, both in Memphis and elsewhere. The flurry of post-war lending sent total loans from $64 million in 1945, to $92 million in 1947.

With business streaming in from both the branches and the correspondent networks, Union Planters grew as never before. Annual profits topped one million dollars in 1943 and continued upward. Capital stock was increased to $4 million, by issuing a $500,000 stock dividend out of retained earnings. And deposits, which had amounted to $93 million in 1941, reached $251 million in 1948.

Those gains moved the bank into select company. According to the *American Banker,* Union Planters' deposits and capital funds placed it seventy-first among the nation's largest banks. Even more impressive was its regional standing; in deposits and capital funds, Union Planters ranked first among all banks in an area covering Tennessee, Kentucky, Arkansas, Mississippi, and Alabama.

Vance Alexander could look back with justifiable pride on what he had achieved during his fifteen years at Union Planters. When he took office the bank had seen better days. It had just gone through four presidents and twenty-one directors in less than four years' time; it was dismissed by some as little more than "a branch of the American National in Nashville"; a group of anxious stockholders wanted to slash capital and close the Manhattan Savings office. Alexander had taken charge of that "fine old rundown institution," as J. C. Bradford wrote, and turned it into the Mid-South's leading bank.[2]

As the 1940s drew to an end, so did the careers of a conspicuously large number of the bank's senior officials. Two key members of the executive committee died: Colonel Canada in 1944, Lytle McKee in 1948. Four other long-time directors also had died: Fred Bianchi (1940), William Loeb (1942), Richard Dozier (1943), and R. G. Bruce (1945). Moreover, a large hole had opened up in the executive ranks. Ike Wilson's right-hand man, Doddridge Nichols, whom many had seen as presidential material, suffered a fatal heart attack in 1947, and Wilson himself was disabled by a chronic illness that would take his life in 1951. That same year, Vance Alexander, now sixty-four years old, decided that the time had come to select the bank's next president.

In sizing up the field of presidential candidates, Alexander looked for someone who could not only maintain the bank's competitive advantage in the Mid-South but also extend its influence over a much wider territory. He believed that Union Planters was poised at the beginning of a "new era," an era during which it might well attain the size and prominence of a Wachovia National or a Citizens & Southern National.

As if to underscore the bank's regional ambitions, Alexander obtained approval, early in 1952, to shorten its name by dropping the words *of Memphis,* which had been in use since 1946. (The words *of Memphis* continued to be used until the early 1980s. however.) And there were other changes aimed at preparing Union Planters for the "new era" of growth. A two-year, $2.3-million expansion of the main office was underway. The building was being raised to nine stories on Front Street and extended down Madison to Center Lane. When completed in April, the enlarged, newly air-conditioned main office occupied a full quarter of a square block.

To add polish and tone to the organization, management opened a private dining room on the ninth floor overlooking the Mississippi River. The daily menu ran to four courses, with "everything made from scratch, even the mayonnaise and ice cream," recalled Mildred Blaine, manager of the dining room for more than twenty-five years. Often said to be "one of the two or three best places in Memphis to eat," the dining room welcomed thousands of the bank's customers over the years, as well as a host of celebrities, including Pablo Picasso, Winthrop Rockefeller, Danny Thomas, Norman Vincent Peale, and Cybill Shepherd.

The dining room was a place where Alexander and his officers could as easily entertain a planter from Tyronza, Arkansas, as the chairman of J. P. Morgan and Company. Alexander was no less exacting in choosing his successor. He might have recommended Executive vice-president and director Milton K. Revill, who had taken over commercial lending and some of the other activities once managed by Ike Wilson. Or he might have settled on the number three man, Executive vice-president Emmett J. House; a director and secretary to the board, House had been given responsibility for the branches and property after Doddridge Nichols' death. Or he might have gone further down into the ranks and picked the head of correspondent banking, John E. Brown, though Brown had been in his position for only four years. Instead, Alexander's search led him out of Memphis, to the Chase National Bank, and to its vice-chairman, Arthur W. McCain.

Born in Little Rock in 1900, Arthur McCain had left the South at an early age, eventually to become an officer in Chase's international division. After service in Argentina, Chile, and Brazil, he had returned to New York as head of the international division. In 1946 he was elected president of the Chase, and remained in that office until being moved to vice-chairman in 1949. Although he was happily settled in Scarsdale, where he served as acting mayor, and though he held the third-ranking post at the world's third largest bank, McCain readily accepted Alexander's offer to "go with the biggest bank in a fast growing region." The board elected him president on April 10, 1952, retaining Alexander as chairman and chief executive.

For his own part, Alexander evidently was intrigued by the prospect of luring a New York banker of McCain's rank to Memphis and Union Planters. He also set great store on the fact that McCain was on a first-name basis with many of the nation's leading bankers. In a memorandum instructing officers how to explain the choice to the public, the bank's management committee emphasized McCain's prominence in banking circles outside Memphis. The memo read in part:

Friends and customers will ask why the bank went outside for a man to succeed Mr. Alexander. [When] Mr. Alexander came to the bank nineteen years ago . . . he brought to us an intimate acquaintance with not only the heads of the banking institutions from coast to coast but also close relationships with a wide number of business leaders all over the nation. These close associations have been invaluable as a contribution to the bank's growth. . . . The selection of Mr. McCain is in no respect a reflection on any of the officers of the bank, since Mr. Alexander and the Board of Directors felt that more than one of our present staff was thoroughly capable. However, because the duties of our top men for many years have required their full time at their desks, circumstances were not always such as permitted them to make the wide associations that the President of our bank should have. We were most fortunate in finding a . . . man [McCain] of varied and seasoned banking experience and who, in addition, enjoyed the national prominence which Mr. Alexander did when he came to Union Planters.[3]

McCain's arrival in Memphis, on May 2, received extensive coverage in the local press. Both newspapers profiled him and his family at length, portraying him as a country boy at heart who had made good as a big city banker and was now returning to his homeland. The *Press-Scimitar,* bursting with civic pride, editorialized:

> Arthur Williamson McCain was a Mid-South boy who made it to the top in the big city—and now the Mid-South will profit by the banking experience and know-how he picked up while he was away. And though he leaves the country's No. 1 city and No. 3 bank, we're sure he will feel quite at home at the president's desk in flourishing Union Planters. For while he was away, Memphis has thrust its head up among the metropolitan cities and is climbing ever more rapidly up the ladder. Already it is the nation's 26th [most populous] city and the Union Planters Bank is already 71st in importance in the nation— and the ceiling is unlimited for both.

Public attention also focused on the grand opening of the bank's enlarged and remodeled main office building, but it was the new president, not the new building, that attracted the most attention. More than one hundred bankers wrote Alexander congratulating him on his choice of McCain. The president of J. P. Morgan and Company, Harry C. Alexander, wrote him: "I think that this [McCain] is a wise step on your part, and although I know that the Union Planters will continue to have all the benefits of your counseling and experience, I trust that in your new position you'll be able to enjoy a little more of the leisure to which you are certainly entitled."

Of all the congratulatory messages, the most colorful one was from Mills B. Lane, Jr., president of Atlanta's Citizens & Southern National Bank. In it, Lane may well have hit on one of the unspoken reasons behind the selection of McCain. "Reading the story of what you have done in bringing in Mr. Arthur McCain," wrote Lane, "I just couldn't help but thrill at what you have done. My father like you was a great believer in training from within and yet he too realized that every once in so often a new bull in the pasture is a fine and healthy thing."[4]

Vance Alexander had moved smoothly from Nashville to Union Planters in 1933, but the transition from Scarsdale to Memphis was none too easy for Arthur McCain. Unlike Alexander twenty-one years earlier, McCain had trouble shedding the image of an outsider. Two years passed as he struggled to establish his authority with the bank's three executive vice-presidents.

In the fall of 1954, Alexander was laid low by a mild stroke. Earlier in the year he had attended the funeral of Ed Crump, the last of the big city bosses. Although Crump had run Memphis as if it were a plantation, his political organization was now leaderless and about to go down to defeat in the mayoral race. Crump had never cared to groom a successor. His enormous power died with him. In many ways, Alexander's authority at Union Planters was nearly as absolute as Crump's had been in Memphis. "Mr. Alec *was* Union Planters," remarked a retired officer. And like Crump, he had provided for almost everything except his own successor. The fate of the Crump organization could only have reminded Alexander of the situation at Union Planters. While recovering from the stroke, Alexander decided to replace McCain.

Vance Alexander's idea of the kind of leader the bank needed had changed entirely over the last four years. He abandoned his earlier belief that the bank needed a president of national prominence and wide-ranging experience. Instead of looking for fresh talent on the outside, Alexander now turned inward, eventually focusing on one of his executive vice-presidents, John Brown. A short, stocky man with heavy jowls and a gruff manner, Brown was widely regarded as one of the best correspondent bankers in the Mid-South. In background and temperament, he was McCain's exact opposite.

Born and reared in Henderson, a small town in the West Tennessee hills,

Brown had passed most of his working career at Henderson's First State Bank, which had been established by his father-in-law, J. F. O'Neal. After O'Neal's retirement in 1937, Brown served as its president. In 1944 he had joined Union Planters' correspondent department, resigned the following year, then returned to the bank in 1948. Three years later, Alexander promoted him to executive vice-president.

At the board meeting of January 13, 1955, the directors voted to shift Arthur McCain into the newly-created post of vice-chairman, which would be left vacant when McCain retired later in the year. Alexander continued as chairman and, on his recommendation, the directors then elected John Brown president. News of his election elated his many banking friends in small towns throughout the Mid-South. According to one newspaper account, Brown soon received "so many calls from his country banking friends that the hundreds of Memphis business leaders trying to congratulate him could hardly get a word in."

CHAPTER 10

Marking Time

This association [with Union Planters]
was a great privilege for a country boy,
even though I never did really understand
you city slickers.
—John Brown to the directors of Union Planters

AUTHORITY passed from Vance Alexander to John Brown gradually, steadily, and without mishap. President Brown frequently acted as the bank's lead spokesman, and he began to preside at meetings of the executive committee when Alexander's health declined in the late 1950s. Even before then, the directors had entrusted Brown with a vital task: find the bank's next president. Although Brown was some ten years away from retirement, the directors wanted his successor in place well ahead of time. Perhaps they considered him an interim president.

Brown scouted the field for over a year before settling on an East Tennessee banker and native-born Memphian by the name of Albert M. "Al" Brinkley, Jr. A tall, patrician man with a knack for bringing out the best in people, Al Brinkley had got his start as a state banking examiner during the Depression, had moved on to the Bank of Maryville, first as cashier and later as president, and then left to join a larger institution, the First National Bank of Kingsport, which he had headed since 1954.

Brinkley was at first reluctant to leave the Kingsport bank. He was well established and in charge there, while at Union Planters he would be understudy to Brown, who was only four years his senior. And unless Brown retired early, Brinkley would be stuck in the number two position at the bank. But Brown eventually persuaded him that Union Planters offered a greatly increased scope for his talents. On February 18, 1958, the board elected Brinkley executive vice-president, at a salary second only to Brown's.

When Brinkley arrived at Union Planters, management was still following the strategy perfected by Vance Alexander in the late 1930s. Retail and correspondent banking remained the primary lines of business. Four new branches had been opened the year before: Frayser and Whitehaven, both on Highway 51; Raleigh, on the Raleigh-Millington Road; and a downtown office at 981 Madison. With thirteen branches in all, Union Planters continued to lead the way in local branch banking. Deposits increased yearly, topping $400 million in 1961, and giving rise to the slogan, "More Memphians Bank At Union Planters Than At Any Other Bank."

Correspondent balances also rose year by year, "holding up tremendously well," said John Brown, even through the ruinous drought of 1957, when inter-bank balances of $79 million accounted for nearly one-third of the bank's total deposits. More than 400 country banks kept accounts with Union Planters in the peak year of 1960, making it the 44th largest "bankers' bank" nation-wide. Officers lavished attention on their customers at the country banks. Said one correspondent officer: "We like to think that we feature all the known inter-bank services, plus a couple that are exclusive to us. If you don't see it, ask for it!" In this field the bank was all but invulnerable to competitors. According to a banker who worked at First National during the period, "there was no way we could compete with John Brown for correspondent business."

The retail and correspondent networks supplied large sums of non-interest bearing funds that could be lent out at rates of from four to six percent, often through the country banks, which bore the costs of originating and servicing the loans. The purchase of discounted paper from automobile dealers and other retailers also provided attractive spreads, allowing the bank to build up its assets without having to incur the expense of developing a large, in-house loan production staff. In such favorable circumstances, Union Planters regularly posted "record level" profits: $3.3 million in 1959, $3.9 million the next year, $4.2 million in 1961.

Although the bank continued to churn out profits, some trouble spots began to appear in 1962. For one thing, correspondent balances plunged to $76 million, compared to $103 million the previous year, and showed no sign of recovering. As country bankers placed fewer dollars with city banks, the correspondent business ceased to be highly profitable. To compensate for the loss, management relied increasingly on its other mainstay, the branch system. Over the next four years the bank would nearly double the number of its branch offices, sharply increasing overhead expenses and straining its capacity to staff all the new offices with experienced managers.

As Brown and his officers shifted resources into the branch system, they encountered a degree of competition they had not seen in the correspondent business. It came from the First National, which was growing at a rapid clip under the leadership of Allen Morgan, elected president in 1961, and board chairman Norfleet Turner, who had worked at Union Planters during the 1920s. With nine branches and $375 million of deposits in 1962, First National was fast closing the gap in size that had long separated it from Union Planters. People who commented on Turner and Morgan's success usually associated it with their ability to develop and motivate officers. A top executive at Union Planters, who worked for Turner and Morgan in the 1960s, recalled:

> The leadership was unbelievable at First National. They were leaders, not managers. . . . Just to be around people like Turner, Morgan, Haizlip, and Billy Mitchell—you almost felt that you owed them something for working there. You would gag at the responsibility they would give you. I look back on the responsibility I had and I think I wouldn't let *anybody* do that now.[1]

John Brown's style of management, by contrast, was not calculated to fill the officers with a sense of mission or stretch their capabilities. Unlike his counterparts at First National, Brown saw little point in recruiting college graduates or devising a training program or setting up a personnel department. Labor-saving machines held no interest for him; in 1966 the bank owned exactly one electric typewriter. Nor did he see any need for an organization chart. But, then, as an officer later pointed out: "We didn't need an organization chart, because everybody reported to John Brown."[2]

Delegating authority down the line did not come naturally to Brown. Almost every decision, regardless how minor, seems to have claimed his personal attention. When the bank's attorneys wanted to use the bank's photocopier, they needed a permission slip signed by President Brown. No other signature would do.

Brown did recognize the dangers of managing Union Planters as if it were a country bank back in his hometown. "I've got to stop running this bank out of my hip pocket," he once confided to a friend. But he never could quite relax his grip. Such matters as the proper way to distribute promotional items, for example, pre-occupied him. There were times when his need for control bordered on the absurd, as in a memorandum he sent to all officers in April 1963, which reads:

Our bank has contracted to purchase a supply of specially designed book matches, and the initial supply has just arrived. Before making them available to the officers, however, we would like to suggest that there are many *effective* ways of distributing them . . . and we want to limit usage with that thought in mind.

In the broadest sense, they were purchased for customers and bank visitors, not for ourselves.

Our contact personnel will probably want to put some in their pockets before making a call. Each officer of the bank may want to keep some in his desk to offer visitors and customers. . . .

Also our supplier furnished us with some gold anodized aluminum containers to hold 25 or 30 books, and it may be that each branch would want to have one of these on a desk or table in the office area for convenience. We would not suggest, however, that it be placed near the tellers or on a check counter.

The matches are packed 50 books to a box and there are 50 boxes to a case. We suggest each branch order a case at a time to minimize handling, remembering, of course, the potential fire-hazard in storage.

Please use the regular Supply Requisition procedure to order them. . . .

If you will help us by remembering that we are after *effective* distribution, we feel confident these matches can do a good job for us.

Brown's cost-consciousness was nowhere more evident than in the matter of compensation. Wages and salaries at Union Planters soon lagged behind those paid by most other banks in the region. At the end of 1961, when the books showed a profit of $4.24 million, Brown asked for salary increases totaling a mere $79,903. More than a few officers saw no increases at all from 1960 through 1968.

Brown's tight-fisted ways saved large sums of money while doing incalculable damage to morale and the overall quality of officers and employees. "John Brown's policies," said a former executive officer, "weren't conducive to keeping anybody worth a damn."

By 1962 the turnover of mid-level managers was drawing fire from the board. According to a director, Brown once responded to their criticism by saying, "It's a wonderful compliment when other banks want our top people. And they'll always be friends with us."

Dissatisfaction spread to the top ranks, as well. Relations between Brown and his designated successor, Al Brinkley, grew chilly. Their differences tended to surface whenever Brinkley showed initiative. There was, for example, the incident of the weighing machine, an antiquated model located in the lobby and used by visitors. Thinking it an eyesore, Brinkley had it replaced with a newer model—only to see the old machine re-appear later in the week on orders given by Brown. Their differences escalated not long after a board meeting in January 1963 when, on the motion of Vance Alexander, who was retiring because of poor health, the directors named Brown chairman and chief executive officer.

A few months later Brinkley handed the board a letter of resignation that bluntly stated his reasons for leaving. "At the beginning of my association with the Bank," Brinkley explained, "I anticipated a more active part in the management policies and expected to assume more assigned responsibilities. While the situation might be best for the Bank, it has not furnished me the personal satisfaction I desire. Neither do I feel that my original purpose . . . is being accomplished."

Brinkley went on to a distinguished career as chief executive of Louisville's Citizens Fidelity Bank & Trust. During his tenure there, deposits climbed from $240 million to $550 million and, according to the magazine *Louisville*, Citizens Fidelity "probably telescoped more innovations into its seven years with Brinkley than in any full decade of its history."

The loss of Brinkley displeased several directors, including Richard A. Trippeer, a dealer in construction equipment who owned a substantial block of Union Planters' stock; C. J. Lowrance, a planter in Driver, Arkansas; and the bank's counsel, Edward P. Russell, grandson of Mississippi's James Lusk Alcorn. In reports presented to the executive committee they repeatedly advocated measures to reduce the talent drain and strengthen the organization. For three years running, they had "consistently reported" that the trust department urgently needed "more personnel to adequately perform its increased work." Nothing came of their recommendations, however; and in 1966 the head of the trust department, Robert N. Lloyd, Jr. joined the exodus of officers, leaving the department with only four "experienced" officers to manage assets having a market value of $215 million.

First National's growth, which had put it almost even with Union Planters, was another sore point with the directors. They urged Brown to get the bank moving again. Feeling the pressure, Brown spent more and more of his time looking over his shoulder at the competition. Staying ahead of First National turned into such a consuming interest that it sometimes appeared to be driving policy, and not always in the most profitable directions. In 1964, as First National prepared to move into a new, 25-story skyscraper on Madison at Third, Union Planters committed roughly $20 million to finance construction of an even taller building, at 100 North Main; plans were made to move the North Memphis branch there and to erect a huge sign, emblazoned with the letters *UP*, atop the building. The effort to upstage First National proved costly, for most of the $20 million had to be charged off.[3] In another instance, management chose to open a branch in a "prestige building," despite the fact that the bank already had two other branches nearby.

Although operations returned a healthy profit of $4.5 million in 1964, the board now insisted that Brown designate a potential successor. He evidently satisfied them by hiring, in February 1965, a 46-year-old loan officer from the First National Bank of Miami, C. Bennett "Ben" Harrison. It happened that Harrison's father, president of an $8 million bank in Milan, Tennessee, was an old friend of John Brown's, which may or may not have had something to do with bringing Harrison to Union Planters. In any event, Harrison scarcely had time to get his bearings when the board, in January 1966, elected him president, while retaining Brown as chief executive.

Harrison's appointment was yet another instance of the bank's inability to develop top-level talent from within. Not since the brief presidency of Gilmer Winston in 1932–1933 had a president come up through the ranks. Of the last nine presidents, going back to Samuel Read, Harrison was the seventh to be brought in from outside.

In addition to his duties as chief operating officer, Ben Harrison was given charge of the loan and credit departments. But that was a lot of territory to cover, and in February 1967, Brown asked Director Cecil Humphreys, president of Memphis State University, to join the bank as vice-chairman. Humphreys would, Brown told the board, "take the administrative burden off Mr. Harrison who would then be the chief loan and credit man." Brown informed the press that he expected Humphreys to accept the post "in the very near future." But Humphreys, when questioned, told reporters that his work at Memphis State had "been a tremendous challenge and it would be hard to leave." More than two months went by while Humphreys pondered his options, privately as well as publicly. Finally, on April 27, he rejected the offer from Union Planters.[4]

Brown might have survived that public snafu, but his fate was as good as sealed in the summer of 1967 when First National supplanted Union Planters as the largest bank in the Mid-South. In August the board called for Brown's resignation, to be effective at the end of 1967.

The board then elected Ben Harrison to the post of chairman and chief executive, while the presidency went to Porter Grace, whose previous role had been confined largely to promoting the bank through his activities as a civic booster and fundraiser.

Ben Harrison faced a daunting array of problems, some obvious, others not. Among the more apparent ones was the demoralized and disintegrating work force. The rate of turnover exceeded thirty-five percent a year, and some of the officers had taken to moonlighting in order to supplement their meager salaries. Harrison acted at once to bring compensation more in line with prevailing rates. During the first six months of his administration, salaries were increased by thirteen percent, in hopes of bringing about "an upturn in employee morale and effort." Besides that, management established a personnel department, launched a recruitment program on college campuses, and introduced an internal newsletter, *Bank Notes*. But salaries still remained substantially lower than those paid by First National, and management struggled to keep the turnover rate at just under thirty percent.

A second group of problems, some of which were not so obvious, involved the haphazard procedures for monitoring accounts. Although match books were strictly controlled, national bank examiners reported that $31 million in loans lacked adequate financial statements and other documentation. And though a ceiling of $150,000 had been set on total overdrafts for several years, they frequently mounted to many times that amount; the excess overdrafts had been criticized by the board's examination committee every year since 1957. Steps were taken to centralize control functions and to computerize information. But the results were mixed. As late as 1969, some payroll records were still being entered by hand into loose-leaf notebooks.

The third problem was how to make better use of resources. Specifically, the bank had over-built its branch system, increasing overhead by adding branches even as average deposits declined. Given this, management switched—or seemed to switch—the emphasis from deposit growth to asset growth. Between 1969 and 1973, loan volume would increase by a staggering 76.9 percent. But this new approach presented difficulties of its own. Among them, as loan growth outstripped deposit growth, the volume of Fed fund purchases rose from $13 million in 1969 to $145 million in 1973. More important, Union Planters was lending enormous sums while troubleshooting the very systems that were tracking those credit accounts.

Committed to an aggressive lending policy—a policy that might enable the bank to overtake First National—Harrison and the board hired a specialist in loan production, James C. Merkle. During three years as president of the First National Bank of Anniston, Alabama, Merkle had increased assets from $43 million to $57.8 million, and earnings from $400,000 to $700,000. Hoping to see similar gains at Union Planters, the board moved Porter Grace to the dormant position of vice-chairman and, in October 1969, named Merkle president.

While President Merkle ran the bank from day to day, Harrison was out and about looking for acquisitions. As a prelude to such deals, banking operations were reorganized as a subsidiary of a holding company, Union Planters Corporation. Three months later, in July 1972, Harrison announced plans to acquire Percy Galbreath & Son, a mortgage banking firm of Union Planters director William Galbreath. Still later in the year, Harrison entered into negotiations to acquire, through merger, Tennessee National Bancshares, a holding company with affiliates in Maryville and Greeneville, Tennessee.

In his annual report of 1972, Harrison suggested that the new year might well bring other acquisitions, which management would reveal at the proper time. As it turned out, there were indeed revelations, but none of the sort that either Harrison or the stockholders expected.

The year 1973 did not begin auspiciously for Union Planters. On March 21, a fire broke out in the basement of the main office. Later in the day, lightning struck the Manhattan branch. Other bolts from the blue struck during the fall and winter. A $305,000 loss was discovered in the bank's trading account. Operations veered into the red during the third quarter, and $6.5 million in loans had to be charged off. As investors watched the bank, four or five times the usual volume of shares changed hands. On November 28, Harrison reassured the public that there was no cause for alarm. "Our house is in order," he said. "We took our lumps in the third quarter of this year. We now have our house in order, and the outlook is bright." But like everyone else, Ben Harrison had no clear idea of the enormous difficulties ahead.

CHAPTER
11

The Rollercoaster Years

*History doesn't repeat itself, but it does
rhyme.*
—Mark Twain

U PHEAVALS at Union Planters tended to come at intervals of fifty
years. In 1874 the directors had ousted President Farrington after discovering that he and a fellow director had borrowed an amount equal to
more than one-third of the bank's entire capital. Fifty years later, in 1924,
unsound lending practices, combined with the inattentiveness of President
Frank Hill and the outright dishonesty of his most trusted executive, had
pushed the bank to the edge of destruction; then, in an effort to shore up
the balance sheet, the stockholders had entangled the bank's affairs with
those of the ill-fated Caldwell and Company. And now, in 1974, Union
Planters was entering a period of crisis remarkably similar to the one
in 1924.

Trouble was apparent on several fronts—trouble stemming in part from
the furious push for business. Not since the Hill administration had management been so open-handed with credit: loan review was weak at best,
loan officers could commit the bank to its legal limit of $7.5 million, and
a major advertising campaign assured the public that at Union Planters,
"Your Name Is Your Collateral."[1]

According to one officer, those and other practices added up to a "marketing philosophy that could be summarized as leverage to the hilt: 'if you get the growth, the profits will come.' Unfortunately, the operating system was inadequate for implementing such a philosophy."[2]

Since 1969, loan volume had ballooned from $377 million to $744 million. But to fund those loans, management had been forced in 1973, when the Fed pushed up interest rates, to borrow heavily at rates in excess of ten percent—while servicing those earlier loans at no more than the ten percent rate fixed by Tennessee's usury law. It was a money-losing situation.

Moreover, a large portion of lendable funds had gone to finance construction projects begun during the real estate boom of 1971–1973. Property values, however, had plunged after the Organization of Petroleum Exporting Countries (O.P.E.C.) quadrupled the price of crude oil in October 1973, and the ensuing recession increased the risks involved in real estate lending. Nonetheless, the volume of real estate loans continued to go up during the spring of 1974.

Unexpected losses had also turned up in the installment credit division. Late in 1972 the division had started to register unusually large losses, mostly on automobile paper bought from local car dealers. According to word picked up on the street by a director of the bank, Union Planters was known among car dealers for taking almost any paper they could produce. Toward the end of 1973, as losses in the division mounted, management had reorganized the division.

Another problem area was the bond investment division, where two officers were let go for "improperly recording transactions." "Sharp restraints" were placed on the division, pending "the implementation of improved procedures and controls."

In the wake of such "disappointing" setbacks, Ben Harrison re-shuffled top management. President Merkle, the official most closely identified with the bank's aggressive lending policies, was let go on November 27, 1973. Six weeks later the board replaced Merkle with George C. Webb, vice-chairman since 1972, who had joined the bank in 1948 during the administration of his father-in-law, Vance Alexander.

The naming of Webb as president evidently was intended to cover up a hole rather than to fix it, for Webb was only two years from mandatory retirement age. And in fact, much of the everyday responsibility of president went not to Webb but to a 38-year-old executive officer, Jesse A. Barr. Barr's superiors thought highly of him, variously describing him as "intel-

ligent . . . congenital . . . hard working . . . very ambitious." His ability
to arrange financing had especially impressed two up-and-coming businessmen, the brothers Jake and C. H. Butcher.

In the late 1960s, Jesse Barr had lent Jake and C. H. Butcher the money
to buy control of a small bank in Lake City, Tennessee, and with his help
the brothers were putting together one of the South's largest banking networks; by 1982—the year Jake Butcher brought the World's Fair to
Knoxville, Tennessee—the Butchers would control more than twenty
banks in two states, as well as a bewildering array of financial subsidiaries.[3] Onlookers marvelled at the speed of the acquisitions, speaking
in terms reminiscent of those applied to Rogers Caldwell and Luke Lea in
the 1920s. "Jake Butcher's going to keep on so that he won't want to run
for governor next time," remarked Tennessee House Speaker (and later
governor) Ned McWherter. "He'll own the whole state. He'll own the
Capitol building. We'll have a drive-in window on the left side of the
thing."[4]

Barr and the Butchers hit it off from the beginning. As Jake Butcher
would say in 1978, "Jesse Barr is the smartest, most loyal, most creative
thinker I've ever known."[5]

Barr had joined Union Planters in 1961, but it was not until the Harri-
son-Merkle administration that his career took off. Between 1969 and
1971, he rose from vice president to a position as head of both the commercial lending and credit departments. With his election in January 1974
as executive vice-president of the Banking Group, which included the
branch system, Barr was the bank's third-ranking executive.

In the spring of 1974, Ben Harrison assured the stockholders that "significant improvements in controls and operating policies and practices are
being implemented" and that "positive steps" had been taken to put the
bank's house in order.[6] But some directors were not so sure of that. One of
the skeptics was Richard A. "Dick" Trippeer, Jr., son of the late director
who had helped bring about John Brown's retirement. Along with a few
other directors, Trippeer concluded that Union Planters—far from being on
the mend—was actually "in deep trouble." In late spring several directors
expressed their misgivings to a major stockholder, Jackson T. "Jack"
Stephens, head of the Little Rock-based Stephens Co., the largest investment banking house off Wall Street.[7]

After hearing the concerns of those directors, Stephens recommended to
the full board that an outside expert be hired to find the bottom line at

Union Planters. He knew just the man: William M. Matthews, Jr. It was an inspired choice at the time.

Stories of Bill Matthews abound. People talk of his ability to carry on two conversations at once, his ferocious stamina and bold flights of imagination, his imperious manner and the almost boyish delight he took in practical jokes and in keeping people guessing. Those who knew him have described him variously as "brilliant . . . intimidating . . . hard-driving . . . a creative genius . . . good at some things and horrible at others . . . uncomfortable with people . . . driven . . . mercurial . . . an enigma." Few people, however, would claim to know Bill Matthews really well. Said one associate: "He has an Oriental mind that works on six or seven levels at a time. You may know what's going on at some levels but not all of them."

Matthews, at age forty-two, was going into his second year as president of the First National Holding Corporation, parent of Atlanta's First National Bank. Although in a top position at one of the region's largest banks, Matthews had grown "disenchanted" there and, characteristically, he was itching for a new challenge. So, when a group of Union Planters' directors asked him, in May 1974, to accept the presidency of the corporation, he readily agreed. Two years later he would say of his decision: "If I had known what I was getting into, I never would have come. But I was here. Because of my family and my ego I [had] to make the best of the situation."

Some observers would maintain, to the contrary, that Bill Matthews was not one to pass up a good fight. That, at least, was the spirit in which he came to Memphis. As if to demonstrate that he meant to stand his ground, he bought one of the city's grand homes, the Kent House, a 9,000-square-foot showplace on South Willet. And he immediately established himself as a public gadfly. Besides criticizing the local utility for not developing sources of alternative energy, he withdrew the bank's direct financial support from the Memphis Chamber of Commerce and pointedly refused to join the sacrosanct Memphis Country Club, explaining to reporters that he had no time for golf.

Nor was he reluctant to voice his opinion of the bank's management over the previous fifteen years. As he told the *Commercial Appeal* in January 1975: "This bank was not professionally run. Fundamentally, we're trying to put in some necessary tools to professionally manage the bank." Openly critical of the Brown and Harrison administrations, Matthews began to assemble a new team of senior executives from the outside.

The only senior-level insider who made the team was executive vice-president James F. Springfield, head of the trust department. Under Springfield's direction since 1968, the trust department had flourished, assets under its management having increased from $215 million to $640 million. The team Matthews was forming would also consist of Rudolph H. Holmes, executive vice-president over personnel, loan administration, and finance; L. Quincy McPherson, who left the presidency of Georgia's First Railroad Bank to take charge of Union Planters' commercial lending, investment, and marketing departments; and Benjamin W. Rawlins, Jr., who would take charge of the operations, data processing and later the retail and consumer lending operations of Union Planters. McPherson and Rawlins had worked with Matthews at the First National Bank of Atlanta.

During the summer and fall of 1974, Matthews and his staff began to get a more accurate picture of the bank's condition. In July an internal probe revealed that the persistent losses from the installment credit division were not merely the result of mistakes, ineptitude, and poor judgment. Rather, several of the division's officers had accepted payments in return for approving credit applications, and some loans had been made to persons who either did not exist or could not be located.[8]

Matthews also learned in May 1974 that the Securities and Exchange Commission (SEC) was threatening to seek an injunction against Union Planters on the basis of information about past activities in the bond investment division that management itself had voluntarily turned over to the SEC. After lengthy negotiations, Matthews was able to settle with the SEC and avoid an injunction.[9]

Other, still larger problems, that had been detected earlier became public knowledge in September. That month, a local grand jury indicted Joseph Harwell, manager of the North Memphis branch, on charges of embezzling $284,000. Even more damaging to the bank, Harwell had granted dozens of questionable loans, totaling over ten million dollars, to Stax Records and related entities. Stax, a pioneer in soul music, had a galaxy of stars under contract in the 1960s: Rufus Thomas, Booker T and the MGs, Otis Redding, Wilson Pickett. And at its peak in 1971, Stax had churned out hit records and huge profits; but more recently the company had fallen on hard times and was unable to pay the accumulated interest on the loans, which Harwell, said the grand jury indictments, had made in return for $100,000 and various other inducements, including expense-paid trips to Las Vegas and Hollywood.

Matthews hired specialists from Atlanta and assigned loan administration officer Morgan Bloomfield to handle the complex negotiations and lit- igation arising from those loans. For a time Union Planters even operated a subsidiary of Stax, which the bank had acquired in foreclosure proceed- ings. But like the cotton plantations Union Planters had ended up with in the 1920s, the recording company could neither be run at a profit nor sold at a price anywhere near what the bank already had tied up in it.

Although Ben Harrison had continued to occupy the post of chairman of Union Planters Corporation, his authority was largely titular and his posi- tion soon became untenable. On October 17, complying with the board's demand, Harrison resigned. The directors then elected Matthews chairman as well as president of the holding company, moved George Webb back to the mainly ceremonial office of vice chairman, and named Dick Trippeer to succeed Webb as president of the bank. Commenting on the reasons be- hind the choice of Trippeer, one director explained: "We were looking for an experienced banker, which Dick wasn't. We were also looking for a man with guts, which Dick did have." Besides that, Trippeer's standing and connections in Memphis made him a valuable spokesman, at a time when public confidence in Union Planters was severely tested.

The $3.6-billion Franklin National Bank of New York was declared in- solvent on October 8, 1974. Its collapse, which was the first major bank failure since the Depression, raised concerns about the health of the na- tion's banking industry. On November 5, less than a month after the Franklin National went under, the *Commercial Appeal* reported that the federal grand jury was conducting an investigation "apparently related to substantial 1973 losses in the bond trading operation" of Union Planters. The news did not raise an outcry, but two days later, on November 7, the executive committee met to consider a report from the Comptroller of the Currency (OCC) which was potentially disastrous to the bank's public image.

Although the OCC and other regulatory agencies had conducted routine examinations of the bank earlier in the year, no regulatory agency had brought to the bank's attention any irregularities in the loan portfolio. But on November 7, the board members learned that the OCC was criticizing some $70 million in loans—a sum greater than the shareholders' equity.[10]

The OCC, following its usual procedure in such cases, requested a meet- ing with the full board to discuss the possibility of issuing a cease and de- sist order against the bank. A cease and desist order, enjoining manage- ment to halt illegal and unsound banking practices, "would have been disastrous for Union Planters" at that point, according to a knowledgeable source.[11] Once it was issued, corporate customers probably would pull their accounts and large depositors would draw down their balances to levels covered by federal deposit insurance.

When the Comptroller's agent met with the directors on November 22, he doubtless had their complete attention. Although no one recorded his remarks, the general tenor was such, said one director, that "a lot of us about fell out of our chairs." The board immediately retained attorneys who were successful in forestalling the order. And Matthews made a forceful case that such an order was not only unnecessary but counter-productive. In the end, the OCC decided not to issue the cease and desist order, even though Union Planters was in some respects in as bad a shape as other banks, such as Hamilton National in Chattanooga, which were ultimately shut down by federal regulators. According to one account, the OCC told Matthews, "in effect, that it did not believe Union Planters would make it, but would give Matthews a chance."[12]

The bank's future looked grim at the end of 1974. Losses for the year amounted to $16.75 million. There were problem loans totaling $62 million, including $48 million in non-performing real estate loans. Stock, which had sold at $21.5 in January, could now be had for as little as $5.25. Bowing to the inevitable, the board voted, on December 10, to suspend the dividend. Since the 1930s, only one or two other large banks had omitted their dividends and survived. Bill Matthews, fearing that the action would trigger a run, arranged for two armored trucks filled with cash to be parked near the bank. They were not needed, though large depositors did start a "silent run," reducing their balances to $100,000 or to amounts slightly greater than their outstanding loan balances. Total deposits slipped from the $1.03 billion of December 1973 to $880.91 million by the end of 1974.

As 1974 drew to a close, Matthews learned of yet another instance where officer infidelity would cost the bank dearly. This time the fraudulent activities involved not just a division manager or branch manager but one of the bank's most senior officers, executive vice-president Jesse Barr. An F.B.I. investigation found that Barr had accepted payoffs for granting dubious or illegal loans of $20 million. In 1976, Barr was convicted of bank fraud and sent to prison. Union Planters obtained a $17.6 million civil judgment against Barr, but, as of this writing, the bank has been unable to collect any part of it.

Bill Matthews also had reason to suspect that Barr was involved in a bid to acquire or take over Union Planters. In 1973, Jake and C. H. Butcher had bought 20,000 shares of Union Planters; other purchases followed, and by January 1975 the Butchers owned at least fifteen percent of Union Planters stock. Like Rogers Caldwell and Luke Lea in the 1920s, the Butchers had sunk a large portion of their assets into Union Planters. But they were seeing no return on the investment now that profits and dividends had vanished. Like Caldwell and Lea, the Butchers had "grabbed hold of an anchor," as Ben Rawlins remarked.

They apparently wanted either to get loose of the bank or else gain working control of it. Toward the end of 1974, Jake Butcher approached another major stockholder, Jack Stephens, and offered either to sell out to Stephens or to buy him out. Stephens wasn't interested. Then, early in January 1975, Jake and C. H. Butcher called on Bill Matthews. Because of their ownership position in Union Planters, they explained to Matthews, they wanted to name two of the bank's directors. Matthews turned them down, telling them that he thought they might be violating federal antitrust laws. To discourage them further, Matthews told them in some detail about the federal investigation of Jesse Barr. "I said these are the acts that Jesse had performed," Matthews remembered, "and I really honed in on a couple of them and asked what their opinion of it was." As Matthews recalled their reaction, Jake Butcher confessed that he really didn't know Jesse Barr that well at all.[13]

Matthews evidently made his point, even if in an oblique way. The Butchers dropped their bid for Union Planters, though they did not drop Jesse Barr. Within a short time Barr became a consultant to the Butchers, working behind the scenes to arrange the acquisition of their flagship bank, Hamilton National Bank of Knoxville (later renamed United American), and making certain that problem loans kept moving from one Butcher bank to another, just ahead of federal examiners.[14] Barr remained faithful till the end, which began on February 14, 1983, when the F.D.I.C. closed United American and when federal authorities were in the midst of investigations that would not only shut down their other banks but also send the Butchers and Barr to prison.

In addition to Barr, at least ten other Union Planters officers were dismissed for misconduct, and most were convicted of criminal charges. In an effort to recover some of the money they had cost the bank, Matthews organized several task forces. The Special Loans Department, directed by James A. Gurley, worked to recover as much as possible of the millions in loans that were charged off. At the same time, the Financial Affairs department, under James A. Cook, Jr., had responsibility for asserting the bank's claims for $16.5 million of restitution on the fidelity bonds of former officers.

By January 1975, the Matthews administration had identified all the areas where the bank was at substantial risk. The hefty losses of the previous year, together with the losses forecast for 1975, strained the bank's capital position. According to one account of the situation, "Matthews had to make certain that the bank's capital position did not fall below $52 million because that would have resulted in legal insolvency."[15] He was able to avoid that by means of an unusual though sound accounting procedure; on the balance sheet he listed a $10 million asset described as "Bond Claims Receiveable." It represented the amount that management felt reasonably certain of collecting from its bonding companies. The item caused the bank's accounting firm to render a "subject to" report, which effectively prevented management from raising capital; but Union Planters remained solvent.

Because capital markets were closed to the bank, Matthews had to shrink assets until they were more in line with existing capital. During 1974 and 1975, management called hundreds of loans, often driving away customers and sometimes angering directors, but nonetheless reducing the loan portfolio from $740 million to $481 million and bringing the capital-to-asset ratio back to a more acceptable level. To cut costs, Matthews sold the 100 North Main building, leased out the bank's dining room, and began to close down marginal branch offices. He also trimmed the workforce by 25 percent, but he raised salaries, believing that low pay scales over the years had contributed to the bank's predicament.

The drive to improve asset quality and the decision to suspend dividends did not always endear Matthews to the stockholders. "I'm sure there are a lot of people who don't like what I've done," he said in January 1975. "We're impacting a lot of people. Many stockholders expected and needed that dividend. . . . [But] someone has to make the unpopular decisions as well as the popular decisions."

At the same time, management was also winning the public relations battle, thanks largely to the policy Matthews and Dick Trippeer followed in dealing with reporters. With memories of the Watergate hearings still fresh, the officials wisely decided not to stonewall or evade questions or experience selective memory lapses. Their policy, as stated by Trippeer, was to be "candid and frank . . . provided such candor does not jeopardize the bank's security or threaten its legal interests."

Their frankness drew praise from several newspapers and publications, including *Business Week, American Banker,* and *Bankers Magazine.* In an article entitled, "How To Deal With Bad News Constructively," the editors of *Bankers Magazine* noted:

> . . . a lesson can be learned from the management of Union Planters Corp., which has had a series of shocks that are the equivalent of anything that has hit elsewhere in the [national banking] system. . . . Throughout its period of turmoil, the Memphis bank has been willing to discuss its problems with the press, rather than avoiding statements or issuing bland, unrealistic announcements suggesting that everything is rosy. . . . Union Planters' openness has probably gotten more favorable information into press coverage than might otherwise have been the case.

By the first quarter of 1976, Matthews had turned a corner. Losses in 1975 had been held to $2.75 million, compared to $16.75 million the year before, purchases of high-cost funds had been sharply curtailed, and there were no unpleasant surprises to explain. "We've set the objectives and criteria for establishing a good, well-run organization," Matthews said. "I can't say they're all working right now. But they're all in place where they ought to work."

The following year, 1977, operations returned to profitability, earning $3.34 million. That summer the Financial Affairs department, working with the bank's law firm, collected $10.8 million on the outstanding bond claims; eventually, total bond collections would far exceed the $10 million "Bond Claim Receivable" asset that Matthews had set up on the 1974 balance sheet. Other significant recoveries were also being made by James Gurley's Special Loan department, which proved adept at collecting previously charged off loans; of the $18.5 million in charge offs occurring between 1977 and 1981, the department recovered $12.1 million, or 65 percent, as against an average recovery rate of 26 percent among comparable banks.

Profits rose to $5.08 million in 1978 and to a record-level $8.77 million in 1979. Business analysts began to speak of the "turnaround" at Union Planters and marvel at the changes wrought by Bill Matthews. Often singled out for mention were the strides made in data processing and delivery systems under the direction of Ben Rawlins. In a report issued in 1981, an analyst at Morgan Keegan called Union Planters the "most technologically advanced bank in the state and region," adding that "most banks still cannot offer key services that Union Planters introduced five years ago."[16] The accomplishments included a system combining information on several account relationships in a single statement to retail customers, and an expanded ATM network, as well as licensing of the Annie machines to twelve banks within a 100 mile radius of Memphis. Those and other technological advances allowed the bank to function in 1980 with about 600 fewer employees than it had had in 1971.

The creation and performance of the Investment Banking Group (IBG) also attracted the notice of analysts. Offering a range of brokerage services, IBG was judged to be "unusually successful," its trading income having grown from $900,000 to $5.6 million between 1978 and 1980.

As a young man, Matthews had aspired to be a Wall Street investment banker. Commercial banking had never captured his fancy, and so it was not surprising that the IBG and the development of other start-up ventures came to absorb much of Matthews' time, to the exclusion of more traditional banking activities. As Rawlins remembered, there came a point when "we seemed to stop developing relationships in the core business of the bank. Bill was selling the bank to analysts as a data processing machine. He was ignoring the bank's historic strengths—lending and retail—in favor of more exotic lines of business."

By 1981, Matthews was increasingly bent on generating profits from trading activities and venture capital projects. His vision of the bank's future was bold. It was grounded in the belief that the very nature of banking had changed and that in order to adapt, Union Planters would have to transform itself into what he called a "merchandizing company." As the 1980 annual report put it:

> Banking has changed. Dramatically. The absence of innovation which characterized the banking industry is a thing of the past, and the year 1980 was the year it became obsolete. . . . A new decade dawned, and the face of an industry was forever altered. . . . Bankwide, we no longer define ourselves in the narrow confines of checking and savings accounts, loans and deposits.

Looking ahead, Matthews envisioned a brave new world of banking in which a lean and hungry Union Planters would compete head on with the nation's largest banks. Union Planters would, said Matthews, "offer costs to customers everywhere in the country and anywhere in the world that no commercial bank can compete with."

The possibilities for profit were "limited only by the ingenuity of the human masters of the systems," for "the world is awash in liquidity looking for work. . . . Our strategy is to extend our computer capacity to the key overseas deposit points from which we can route this excess liquidity back to the United States. From Memphis, we can offer this high-powered, high-velocity multinational pool of liquidity[,] cost economies not dreamed of at their home bases, which the major metropolitan banks can't begin to match. . . . We can cover the entire world from Memphis."[17]

Matthews was no longer speaking of Union Planters in terms that most bankers could readily comprehend. Like most highly creative individuals, Matthews was intrigued by possibility and potentiality, so that at times it seemed that he thought of Union Planters the same way Orson Welles had thought of Hollywood. On seeing a movie studio for the first time, Welles quipped, "It's the biggest train set a boy ever had."

Matthews also invested large sums in state-of-the-art transaction processing systems, which were given names such as Sandman, Prophet, and InnoVision. A staff of 120 was hired to develop and market InnoVision to banks in the region. Some of the new services, such as the electronic fleet control system for the trucking industry, eventually became quite profitable.

Not all the executives were comfortable with the sheer number of those start-up enterprises and the emphasis placed on them. "To be quite honest," Matthews told an interviewer in 1982, "some of our management people are in a state of shock right now, because everything is changing so rapidly and our organization is taking on so many non-traditional functions."

The extent of the dissatisfaction with the bank's direction became evident in September 1982, when Executive vice-president Ben Rawlins and Vice-chairman Quincy McPherson abruptly resigned. After their departure, Matthews seemed to withdraw further into himself. "He began," said Dick Trippeer, "to make all the decisions without anybody having the opportunity to say no. He became a one-man show."

"Key overseas deposit points . . . high-velocity multinational pool of liquidity"—not many of the directors could follow that line of thought. But Bill Matthews had never been far off base. And he was, after all, the man who had stepped in and saved the day in 1974 when, to quote one observer, "Union Planters was about to fall off into the river." And so, the board approved his plan to introduce transactional banking in Memphis. Union Planters thus became the first bank not only in Memphis but also in the Southeast to adopt explicit pricing, which meant that customers were charged for basic services such as check processing. Although explicit pricing boosted fee income, it also lost the bank some 12,000 local customers, who balked at paying for services that, by tradition, were supposedly free.

In May 1983, when the banking empire of Jake and C. H. Butcher fell into the hands of F.D.I.C. receivers, Union Planters bought two of the unit banks: United American Bank of Nashville and United American Bank of Chattanooga. While the acquisition gave Union Planters a foothold in both East and Middle Tennessee, it also negatively impacted earnings by $5.5 million at a time when profits from traditional banking operations were running millions of dollars below the previous year's mark, and a new subsidiary, Union Planters Associates, which specialized in raising venture capital, was not doing as well as expected. Earnings fell, and at year's end management reported a profit of only $4.35 million; but a large part of that amount had come not from operations but from gains achieved through the sale of the main office building at 67 Madison.

Despite the sharp downturn in earnings, the poor results in conventional banking operations, and the losses coming from some of the high-tech subsidiaries, Matthews stuck to his program of change and innovation. He saw no reason to compromise with his vision of the future. As Ben Rawlins later commented: "Bill wouldn't go from his concept of what would happen in the future to the question of how to get through the next few years." In the spring of 1984, management sent the stockholders an annual report that, at first glance, could have been mistaken for the annual report of a robotics company. Pictured on the front cover was "UP4U," a four and one-half foot, two-hundred-pound promotional robot with moveable arms and rotating head dome. "In 1984," the report stated, "UP4U will travel across the state to meet employees and customers, and will make numerous public appearances promoting new products and services. Before long, UP4U may become a widely recognized symbol of Union Planters."

Operations went deeper into the red during the first and second quarters of 1984, but Matthews held to his course. He told the press that he was thinking of dismembering Union Planters, taking it apart and selling its one profitable division, the IBG, or maybe even selling the bank itself. "I'm looking at every unit," he explained. "Because of the problems of 1974–75, I had to rebuild the bank. Some of those units have become [spin off] opportunities to make money for the stockholders." Competitors wondered if Matthews was onto something they had overlooked. As Robert

Booth of C & I Banks said at the time, "He's either real right and we're all wrong, or he's horribly wrong."[18]

Matthews was "tired of it all by then," said a close associate, who agreed that Bill Matthews was the sort of banker who could do the impossible but found it difficult to get through an ordinary business day.

The directors also were tired of it all. They were not prepared to wait and see whether Matthews was about to slip on a banana skin or pull a rabbit out of his hat. On September 27, 1984, they asked for his resignation and he obliged them.

As his successor, the board elected Ben Rawlins. The program agreed upon by Rawlins and the board called for a return to basics. "It is our intent," Rawlins told the stockholders at the next annual meeting, "to recommit ourselves to traditional banking services. We will re-emphasize, strengthen, and restore credit-based and depository banking services, the cornerstone of the organization for over 100 years."

CHAPTER 12

Striking A Balance

The fox knows many things, but the hedgehog knows one big thing.
—Archilochus

BEN RAWLINS accepted a difficult assignment when he became chief executive of Union Planters in the fall of 1984. Rawlins was the third man to hold that office since 1974, and both of his immediate predecessors had been let go by the board. Despite the talk of a "turnaround" in the late 1970s, the bank's strategic direction was as unsettled in the fall of 1984 as it had been in the spring of 1974.

Rawlins took charge of Union Planters at a time when the bank had been veering from one extreme to another for almost thirty years. Beginning in the late 1950s, John Brown had run Union Planters as if it were a small country bank. But during the late 1960s his successor, Ben Harrison, had delegated authority with both hands and watched as the stops were pulled out of lending. Then Bill Matthews, after steering the bank out of grave danger, had turned it in the direction of merchant and investment banking to the bewilderment of many employees and customers.

Rawlins intended to find a middle way between those extremes. For him that meant a return to "basic core banking," shifting from short-term investments to loans and placing the emphasis on "developing business relationships" rather than on purely transactional banking. He felt that reports of the death of conventional banking were greatly exaggerated. "A lot of people believe that traditional banking is dead," he remarked in 1994. "The banking industry has lost market share, but it's a long way from dead. History has a habit of repeating itself, and this is part of a cycle. We do business differently than before, but the difference is more a matter of form rather than of substance. This is still a relationship business. Essentially, it is a personal business."[1]

Traditional lending and depository functions had been neglected for three years or longer. Between 1973 and 1983, total loans had barely increased at all, going from $744 million to $838 million; and deposits at the end of 1983 amounted to $1.04 billion, as compared with $1.03 billion at the end of 1973. During 1984 the only significant profits at Union Planters were coming from its Investment Banking Group (IBG). But IBG's profit of $11.1 million in 1984 was wiped out by heavy losses elsewhere, including the $22 million operating loss in the bank itself. Moreover, the books showed non-performing assets of $60 million and reserves of only $10 million. Regulators were once again concerned about the bank's capital position.

What had been done during the first three quarters of 1984 and even before then could not be undone in the final quarter. At year's end the bank reported a net loss of $18.78 million.

The losses ate into equity and reserves. At the recommendation of the Office of the Comptroller of Currency (OCC), the board signed a letter of agreement that called for Union Planters to increase its capital-to-assets ratio from 4.59 percent to at least 6.5 percent. The board also agreed to suspend the dividend for so long as the ratio remained below 6.5 percent.[2]

Rawlins began writing off non-traditional operations and doubtful assets. Besides folding up InnoVision and similar ventures, he charged off $3.6 million in loans to Mexico and Nicaragua, closed some branch offices outside Memphis, and trimmed $6 million from overhead by cutting 200 positions out of the payroll. In a move to bolster the capital structure, $30.73 million in debentures was placed during 1985. The private sale added $21.27 million to capital.

Early the same year, Rawlins brought in the first key member of his executive team, J. Armistead "Army" Smith. A native of Corinth, Mississippi, Army Smith had been with First Tennessee (formerly First National) for 25 years, serving in various capacities including president of unit banks in Kingsport, Maryville, and Knoxville. Smith was given the task of repairing commercial and retail operations at Union Planters. That,would take time, Smith told Rawlins. "Don't expect a long-bomb quarterback," he said. "What we're going to have to do is a kind of three yard, cloud of dust program."[3]

Rawlins himself devoted much of his time to mastering the layers upon layers of financial complexity that had been put in place during the Matthews administration. As Rawlins remembered: "There were so many moving parts, we just didn't know if we'd done enough to get it back into profitability." His analysis of the inner mechanisms was, however, accurate enough to produce small gains by year's end: commercial banking operations returned a profit of $3.6 million. That profit, together with the much greater one of $13.1 million generated by IBG, allowed Union Planters to close out 1985 with earnings of $11.2 million—a record year for the company.

The steady, incremental gains added up. Earnings in 1986 rose to $19.1 million, with the commercial bank supplying $5.6 million of that amount. Average deposits were also on the rise again—up $100 million over 1985—and average loans had climbed by $149.3 million during the same period. And the capital-to-asset ratio, after hovering around the required 6.5 percent, reached a stable, clearly acceptable level. Toward the end of 1986, when capital amounted to 8.2 percent of assets, the OCC released Union Planters from the consent agreement, whereupon the board reinstated the dividend in February 1987.

With annual results improving by 1987, Rawlins and the board were able to give more thought to positioning Union Planters for the future. Their overriding goal was to build a solid foundation for expansion, to broaden and strengthen the earnings base, or as Rawlins put it, to obtain "multiple sources of stable income." As matters stood, income came from just two main sources: commercial operations in Memphis, which could not grow at a rate much greater than the modest rate of growth predicted for the local economy, and the extraordinarily profitable IBG. As the bank's leading profit-maker, the IBG had contributed more than 40 percent of total revenues and more than 70 percent of total profits in both 1985 and 1986. But the IBG was riding high on a bull market that was bound to collapse sooner or later. When the tremendous demand for fixed-rate securities—fuelled by deregulation of the thrift industry—came to an end, the torrent of profits from IBG could easily vanish overnight.

That prospect did not enhance the marketability of Union Planters shares. "In bank stocks, investors don't like volatile earnings," Rawlins said. Accordingly, he planned to "reduce over time the percentage of earnings contributed by . . . broker-dealer operations [IBG, etc.] to about 30 percent of total earnings." To develop fresh and more predictable income streams, Rawlins embarked on a program of acquiring community, or country, banks having clean balance sheets and consistently high earnings. No single acquisition would significantly affect Union Planters, but collectively the community banks would become the major impetus for growth.

In many respects, the acquisition program was a modern version of the strategy employed by the Alexander administration of connecting Union Planters into a vast network of downstream correspondent banks during the 1930s and 1940s. Rawlins, by building the bank's franchise through a series of small acquisitions, was choosing the dependable if unspectacular approach to growth rather than the glamorous but less secure one offered by securities trading and merchant banking. During July and August of 1986, Union Planters entered into agreements to purchase its first three community banks, all of which were located in Middle and East Tennessee: the Bank of Roane County in Harriman, First Citizens Bank in Hohenwald, and First National Bank in Crossville. Those acquisitions added $383 million in assets and $26 million in equity.

In April 1987 the bottom fell out of the bond market, and the IBG, which had cleared $16.2 million the year before, barely broke even. The adverse effect, however, was minimized by gains achieved in traditional commercial banking—which contributed $11.4 million in operating profits, or nearly double the amount of 1984—as well as by earnings from the three acquired institutions.

According to the 1987 annual report:

Each of the acquired banks performed in line with expectations on an earnings per share basis and did well in comparison with banks of similar size. In the aggregate, they produced a return on assets of more than 1 percent and a return on equity of over 15 percent.

By 1988 Rawlins was close to assembling a full team of senior executives. In addition to Army Smith, Rawlins had recruited a former officer of First Tennessee, Kenneth W. Plunk. With IBG's profits reduced to a trickle, the need for alternative sources of income became more pressing. Plunk would head the expanding group of community banks to help make up the shortfalls. Under his direction, the community banks retained their original names and continued to operate "pretty much as free-standing institutions," as Plunk would later say.[4] Another newcomer was Robert L. Booth, Jr., one-time chief executive of Commerce Union Bank and later of Memphis' Boatmen's Bank. Named chief financial officer in 1989, Booth would also serve during 1990 and 1991 as head of the group of urban banks radiating out from Nashville and Chattanooga.

When Booth arrived at Union Planters in October 1988, the bank was preparing to close out the most profitable year in its history. Earnings hit a record level $25.6 million, and many analysts were saying that the bank was well along the road to recovery. "A symbol of UP's recovery," noted the *Commercial Appeal*, "will be the listing next month [February 1989] of Union Planters shares on the New York Stock Exchange." Analysts also commented favorably on the acquisition program, which was extending the bank's holdings into Mississippi. A presence in Mississippi was established in February 1989 with the acquisition of United Southern Corporation, a $345-million, multi-bank holding corporation that had grown out of the Bank of Clarksdale, established by former Union Planters president Ed Peacock.

The purchase of United Southern was one of the first steps in what initially came to be known as the "Delta Strategy." As Robert Booth explained in 1990: "Our strategy is to stay within a 150-mile radius or so of Memphis with community banks, and with suburban or urban banks we'll go as far as 300 miles. That takes in a number of cities like St. Louis, Little Rock, Jackson [Mississippi], and Nashville." The Delta Strategy, particularly as it related to community banking in the Memphis trade region, put Union Planters back in touch with its historical strengths; in place of Bill Matthews' drive to transform the bank into a major recycler of petrodollars, Rawlins was focusing on the country banks with which the Alexander administration had formed such highly profitable relationships. This time around, instead of being downstream correspondents, the country banks such as the Bank of Clarksdale were becoming affiliates of Union Planters.

To round out his management team, Rawlins selected Jackson W. Moore, a 40-year-old attorney with the bank's law firm. Rawlins had gotten Moore to join the board two years earlier. In April 1989, Moore was elected president of the corporation, Army Smith was elected vice-chairman, and the board re-elected Ben Rawlins as chief executive with the additional title of chairman. Besides his legal expertise and close working relationship with Rawlins, Moore had extensive experience with country banks, having for some years been the largest stockholder of a $75-million bank owned by his family in Clanton, Alabama, as well as a director of an Arkansas banking corporation owned by his father-in-law, Kemmons Wilson, founder of Holiday Inns.

Union Planters went into Alabama during June 1989, with the acquisition of the $18-million Steiner Bank in Birmingham. The deal's significance was long-term, as a potential building block. According to an analyst with Morgan Keegan: "It's not a big deal size-wise. It's important, though, because it's [Union Planters'] first entry, and the first entry by any Tennessee bank . . . into Alabama." Efforts were also underway to enter Arkansas, efforts that would culminate in the acquisition of the $421-million North Arkansas Bancshares in 1990.

In most other respects, however, performance in 1989 fell far short of the expectations generated by the banner year of 1988. With a year-end loss of $22.3 million, earnings were "obviously off track," Rawlins told the shareholders, adding that the results "were disappointing for me personally."[5]

The poor showing was not, however, symptomatic of widespread internal trouble of the sort experienced in 1974. Rather, it was largely the consequence of problems in two areas. For one thing, the securities market was still reeling from the 1987 debacle, which in turn led to extreme problems among the thrift institutions from which the IBG derived more than two-thirds of its income. As a result, the IBG lost $3.6 million on operations.

The other problem occurred in the loan portfolio. Around mid-year, management recognized that serious "credit quality problems" had developed. To build loan volume, the bank had extended credit to borrowers who were involved in commercial real estate and leveraged buy-out syndications. Slightly more than $30 million was tied up in eight loans now recognized as problems. According to one internal estimate, $7 million in charge-offs would have to be made. Since that amount, together with the $3.6 million operating loss from IBG, would destroy earnings for 1989, Rawlins and Smith decided to clear the books of other doubtful loans, some of which had been carried since 1974. Their idea was to "get it over with," to "take our licks," thereby confining unusual charge-offs to 1989 so that there would be "no surprises in 1990." They eventually charged off $47.9 million, or 2.3 percent of total loans in 1989, and they set up an $11.7 million reserve for legal fees and litigations expenses in connection with suits brought against Union Planters by former customers of the IBG.[6]

News of the 1989 loss sent the price of shares tumbling and again caused talk in financial circles of the bank's "erratic earnings history" and "erratic track record." But several analysts praised management for taking the long view rather than attempting to produce short-term earnings at any cost.

Joseph Stieven, of Stifel, Nicolaus & Company, concluded that, "while the charges are disappointing, we believe it sets the company on a firm base going forward." An analyst with J. C. Bradford expressed similar thoughts: "The community banks have all been acquired on terms that have been additive to current and future earnings. The net loss reported during 1989 is the result of aggressive reserve building and the write off of purchase-related intangibles. These two steps, as well as current plans to restructure the company's broker dealer operations all bode well for future earnings."[7]

Rawlins noted that, despite the setback,

> Union Planters came out of the decade a much larger and stronger organization. We ended 1989 with slightly more than $4 billion in assets, $2.1 billion in loans and $3.1 billion in deposits. Our nonperforming assets are at the lowest level in a decade, while general reserves are at the highest level. Overall quality measures are sound. Our capital strength is excellent with total capital of approximately $354 million. We have the largest loan and deposit market in many, if not most, of the markets we serve. With those solid fundamentals the Corporation is well positioned as we enter the decade of the 90's.

To a large degree, the financial crunch of 1989 can be seen as a test of management's oft-stated commitment to conservative banking principles. Instead of papering over the problems, the Rawlins administration acknowledged them and took corrective action. Doubtful loans were purged before they could become an issue with regulators. In-house lending limits were reduced, with loan amounts in excess of $1 million requiring approval by the loan committee. Participation in highly-leveraged transactions and national lending syndicates was drastically curtailed in favor of consumer lending in markets closer to home.

The challenge posed by the reversal of 1989 was, in Rawlins' view, "not just to get earnings back on track but to *stabilize* earnings." It represented an opportunity to "purify our earnings and our balance sheet," he said. In addition to reorienting loan policies, executive management took a close look at the turbulent IBG. Many of its brokerage clients, and most of its profits, had come from savings and loan institutions which, after a heyday in the mid-80's, were floundering as the thrift industry entered a period of crisis. Not only had IBG's client base eroded, but its activities had also spawned a growing number of lawsuits, most contending securities fraud. The annual report of 1989 listed no fewer than eight lawsuits stemming from broker-dealer activities and seeking more than $200 million in damages. There was little hope of speedy settlements. In fact, it seemed likely that the corporation would become entangled in protracted, costly litigation; as other former clients in the thrift industry went into receivership, management at Union Planters expected that "litigation costs will increase given the Resolution Trust Corporation's . . . announced propensity for litigation involving failed savings and loan institutions." Attorneys' fees related to the lawsuits ran to $1.6 million in 1989 and $1.3 million in 1990.[8]

Under the circumstances, Rawlins decided that "an exit from direct participation in the broker-dealer business" was imperative. During the fall of 1990, IBG was dismantled, and in January 1991 the bulk of its operations were placed in a limited partnership formed with another Memphis broker-dealer. The divestiture of IBG greatly reduced the bank's exposure to market fluctuations and litigious customers from that point on. But the costs of resolving lawsuits already filed would be an impediment for at least two years longer; litigation expenses and settlement costs ran to $8.6 million in 1991 and to $11.3 million in 1992.[9]

By the end of 1990, however, the community bank subsidiaries were supplying a large new source of income that more than compensated for the high costs of defending IBG-related suits. Since 1986, Union Planters had acquired eighteen community banks with combined assets of $1.7 billion; seventeen of the eighteen banks held either first or second place in deposit market share in their respective trade areas. As a group, those institutions were the corporation's most profitable segment of business, contributing $15.7 million toward total earnings of $22.7 million in 1990.

The Community Banking Group (CBG) continued to be a leading and reliable performer. Out of total earnings of $27.5 million in 1991, the CBG supplied $21.1 million. Moreover, Union Planters' asset quality, liquidity, and capital ratios had improved markedly since the slump of 1989. At the end of 1991 there were reserves of $47.9 million to cover non-performing loans amounting to $30.3 million, and capital adequacy exceeded the new regulatory minimums that banks were required to attain by the end of

1992. As a result of those and other indicators, a study commissioned by the *U.S. Banker* ranked Union Planters fourth among the nation's largest bank holding companies in safety and soundness.

Building on that solid base, management expanded the franchise substantially in 1992, particularly along Interstate 40 which runs across Tennessee from Memphis through Nashville and Knoxville. During the last week of March, Union Planters acquired Fidelity Bancshares, a $822-million savings and loan based in Nashville, and also purchased $585 million in deposits of Metropolitan Federal Savings and Loan, a failed Nashville thrift with seventeen branches. After the integration of those two branch systems with the lead bank in Memphis, Union Planters ended up with twenty-two branch locations in Nashville, the fastest growing market in Tennessee, and a larger presence in Knoxville and Jackson, the third and fifth largest markets in Tennessee. With only three branches in Nashville at the start of the year, Union Planters wound up with nearly 14 percent of Nashville bank deposits by April 1992.

The statewide expansion was accompanied by a realignment of senior management in which Armistead Smith and Ken Plunk switched assignments. In March 1992, Plunk was named president of Union Planters Bank and its regional subsidiaries, replacing Smith, who became head of the Community Banking Group of separately chartered organizations in Alabama, Arkansas, Mississippi, and Tennessee.

Two new banks entered the CBG fold during 1992: the $90-million Bank of Commerce in Woodbury, Tennessee, and Southeast Bancshares, parent of the $80-million DeKalb County Bank and Trust in Alexandria, Tennessee. At the end of 1992, the CBG consisted of twenty-one banks that showed an excellent return of 1.36 percent on average assets. The program of acquisition boosted corporate assets from $3.8 billion to $5.2 billion in 1992. Earnings that year rose to $41.4 million, while quality standards remained exacting. The emphasis on quality and security was obvious as reserve coverage increased to $64.3 million, or 194 percent of non-performing loans. That level of coverage was one of the highest among hundreds of banks in Union Planters' peer group, and the percentage of non-performing loans was among the lowest in the group.

By the end of 1992, analysts noted that a transformation was in full swing at Union Planters. According to Kay Lister of Keefe, Bruyette & Woods, Union Planters had "successfully re-engineered itself away from a company whose earnings were highly dependent on the fortunes of the broker/dealer subsidiary in favor of building a profitable community banking network across Tennessee and into the neighboring states of Arkansas, Mississippi, and Alabama." That sort of strategic initiative was unusual among Tennessee banks, in the view of *BankWatch,* which observed:

> Unlike its Tennessee peers—which are [either] traditional banking companies imbedded in the community, aggressive players seeking new business opportunities similar to banking, or struggling institutions challenged by asset quality problems—UPC created and pursued an identity that focused on maintaining a lead bank subsidiary surrounded by community banks and thrifts, each having good management and holding a significant market share in its local area.[10]

The quickening pace of development continued in 1993, leading one observer to conclude that Union Planters was "the fastest growing bank in Tennessee."[11] From January 1993 to January 1, 1994, Union Planters completed no fewer than thirteen acquisitions. Among them were the Bank of East Tennessee in Morristown, SaveTrust Federal in Dyersburg, First Federal Savings in Maryville, Garrett Bancshares in Goodlettsville, Hogue Holding Company in Weiner, Arkansas, and Mid-South Bancorp in Franklin, Kentucky. Together they added some $1.5 billion to assets and enlarged the CBG to thirty-five banking subsidiaries. The CBG now held several times more assets than the entire Union Planters organization had held in 1984. And the statewide branch system administered from Union Planters Bank in Memphis had grown to the point where stand-alone banks could be formed in several metropolitan areas. In November 1993, the board made plans to charter four new Union Planters banks, headquartered in Chattanooga, Jackson, Knoxville, and Nashville, Tennessee.

With most of its litigation troubles out of the way and revenue flowing in from affiliates in five states, Union Planters began to demonstrate its earnings potential in 1993, generating a profit of $61.2 million that year. At the same time, a closely watched index of bank performance showed significant improvement: the return on average assets rose to 1.01 percent, or just above the industry benchmark of 1 percent.

Commenting on the outlook for Union Planters, Henry Coffey, Jr. of J. C. Bradford & Co. wrote:

> Under Ben Rawlins . . . Union Planters has established a history of financial discipline. For a number of years, the focus had been moving away from volatile sources of earnings [and toward] serving the

region's small business and consumer market. . . . Approximately half of pretax earnings are now generated by the community banks, and the litigation costs associated with the company's broker/dealer operation are now behind it. . . . Management has successfully built an earnings stream that should prove to be both highly predictable and profitable.

Indeed, the shift in direction at Union Planters had brought gains as substantial as any achieved since the early and middle years of the Alexander administration. Between March 1984 and March 1994, assets had climbed from $1.9 billion to $6.7 billion, deposits had grown from $1.4 billion to $5.7 billion, shareholder equity went up from $75 million to $513 million, and loan volume expanded from $876 million to $2.9 billion while non-performing loans decreased from $60 million to $27 million and the loan-loss reserve increased from $10 million to $80 million. From what was essentially a one-bank, one-county operation with a huge investment banking business in 1984, Union Planters had developed into a multi-bank holding company with a statewide branch system and a network of thirty-five subsidiaries extending from the Ozarks to the Appalachians.

In many ways, the changes wrought at Union Planters were symbolized in a new headquarters building that was completed in the early spring of 1994. The old home office, on the riverfront at 67 Madison, which the bank first occupied in 1924, had not seen a major renovation since 1952. Much of its original grandeur had been lost in piecemeal remodelings during the intervening years; many interior spaces, particularly the main banking room, were visually unattractive combinations of design elements that had been cobbled together over the decades with little regard for balance, harmony, and overall effect on the viewer.

In addition to those aesthetic drawbacks, the building's location had become less desirable as more of the bank's customers migrated eastward to suburban and commercial areas many miles distant from the city center. Although it was apparent that any move away from downtown would be seen in some quarters as an act of civic disloyalty, management decided to relocate the main offices of Union Planters in new buildings closer to its customers.

During the latter part of 1991, most of the main office staff had moved from 67 Madison to a newly-constructed, $17-million administration building situated alongside Interstate 40 in the Memphis suburb of Cordova. Then, during the winter of 1992, ground was broken for the bank's new headquarters building. The site chosen, which was said to be among the most valuable pieces of undeveloped real estate in Shelby County, was at 6200 Poplar Avenue, close to the population center of greater Memphis and near one of the busiest intersections in the state.

On that site in March 1994, workers completed construction of a four-story, $10 million building that could have been mistaken for a Federal Reserve Bank or the Tennessee State Capitol. Designed in Greek Revival style, with a granite base, massive columned facade, and a large hip roof of copper, the building was a virile statement of Southern culture and economic attainment. It projected an image of invulnerability and stood out like a landmark amid the welter of sleek but faceless office complexes and corporate centers along the Poplar corridor. Inside the main lobby, which soared up two stories in height, architectural features such as coffers, vaults, columns, pilasters, and an enormous chandelier suggested a grand banking hall dating from the mid-nineteenth century.

Monumental in scale and timeless in design, the new headquarters building was an eye-catching sign of the bank's heritage. Since 1869, Union Planters had been open every business day without fail. During those 125 years, the bank had weathered changes that altered the very fabric of society. Union Planters had endured and prospered in the worst of times as well as in the best of times, through wars and depressions, booms and panics, ever since before the yellow fever.

Notes and Sources

ABBREVIATIONS

ESC	Wilson and Ferris, eds. *Encyclopedia of Southern Culture*
ESH	Roller and Twyman, eds. *Encyclopedia of Southern History*
HGFP	Hill-Grosvenor Family Papers
MCA	*Memphis Commercial Appeal*
MCCJ	*Memphis Chamber of Commerce Journal*
MPL MR	Memphis-Shelby County Public Library, Memphis and Shelby County Room
MPS	*Memphis Press-Scimitar*
MSRD	*Memphis Social Register and Directory, 1925*
MSU MVC	Memphis State University, Mississippi Valley Collection
RC BL	Rhodes College, Burrow Library
RTP	Robertson Topp Papers
SHC	Southern Historical Collection, University of North Carolina at Chapel Hill
TSLA	Tennessee State Library and Archives
UPNB	Union Planters National Bank, Archives
WTHSP	*West Tennessee Historical Society Papers*
WWT	*Who's Who in Tennessee, 1911*

(See Bibliography for full citations)

1. FORTUNES OF WAR

On ante-bellum business and finance in Memphis: Greider, Keating (vols. 1 and 2); Redlich; Sigafoos; Ballaugh, *The South in the Building of the Nation* (vol. VI).

On the Battle of Memphis (June 6, 1862): *Battles and Leaders of the Civil War* (vol. 1); Capers; Grant; Harkins; *Historical Times Encyclopedia of the Civil War*.

On Commerce in Memphis, 1862–1865: Blotner (vol. 1); Cohn; Coulter; Hallum; McPherson; Parks; RTP: RC BL; Sigafoos.

1. Steamboats: Hallum; McIlwaine; Sigafoos; Twain.
    According to Hallum, blockade runners were able to obtain insurance coverage. Relating his own experience, Hallum writes: "I also told him [steamboat captain Malone] that I could at once charter the boat for $30,000 for 12 months, with insurance and repairs . . ."
2. William Farrington and Robertson Topp: MCA, February 18, 1911; Keating-Vedder (vol. 2); "Minutes of Meeting of the Board of Directors of Cossitt Library, November 15, 1911," MPL MR; McIlwaine; Sigafoos.
    By far the most important source consulted was the collection of Robertson Topp Papers at Burrow Library, Rhodes College, Memphis. As those documents show, Topp trafficked in goods between enemy lines. To do so he at first played a double game, offering his allegiance to both sides. On July 31, 1861, Alexander M. Clayton wrote Jefferson Davis in Topp's behalf, saying that Topp had "lately spent some time in East Tennessee . . . endeavoring to bring about harmony and unanimity in that [pro-Union] region [and is] now thoroughly identified in the feelings and with the actions of the Confederate states." And yet, on October 1, 1861, William G. Brownlow wrote Topp thanking him for his help in keeping East Tennessee a pro-Union stronghold.
    Later, as the military advantage went to the North, Topp spoke openly in support of the Union. With the help of powerful friends, he was able to trade between the lines throughout the war. One military governor of Memphis, General S. A. Hurlburt, whom the Topps entertained at their home on Beale Street, sent a naval expedition down the Red River, in November 1863, for the purpose of bringing out cotton owned and stored there by Topp and his brother-in-law, William L. Vance.
    In February 1864, Topp was in Washington, D.C., trying to secure special trading permits for himself. As he wrote in a letter of April 10, 1864, on stationery of the U.S. House of Representatives:

> "As yet we have done nothing. Mr. [Lincoln] had three meetings of cabinets, but every time Stanton [Edwin M., Secretary of War] put in some damper. We have given up the General Permits as hopeless. Nearly so— the special order for myself.

> "Have some hope of getting a letter to [name scratched out] requesting him to let out all produce in the name of Burbridge [?]. This is the way things are done. We make friends with the military. Indirectly many things are obtained. I have some hopes of getting a private note from L [Lincoln] to military commanders but may not.

> "If Stanton was out of the way I could have succeeded long ago. . . . I will go back to New York for capital.

"Cossitt [see footnote 2 to Chapter 4] says if I can get any paper that promises well an arrangement can be made with Brown & Brown [now Brown Brothers Harriman] for all the money needed. . . ."

Through Senator Henry Clay, Topp did obtain an appointment with President Lincoln. He asked Lincoln for a "private note to military commanders" instructing them to assist in moving 300,000 bales of cotton out of the Mississippi Delta. Lincoln declined, explaining that "Col. Topp must take his chances with the others, without any special exception." But on October 22, 1864, Lincoln issued an order to military commanders instructing them to offer "such protection and such facilities of transportation and otherwise . . . as can be conveniently done within the Regulations of trade and within the public service" to James Hughes of Indiana. Hughes thereupon appointed Topp his agent. Through intermediaries such as Hughes, O. H. Burbridge, and William L. Vance, Topp also obtained special trading permits from General U. S. Grant (February 25, 1865) and from President Andrew Johnson (April 24, 1865). RTP: RC BL.

3. William Wood and Samuel Read: MCA, February 9, 1915; HGFP: SHC; Keating (vol. 2).

4. Napoleon Hill's early life: HGFP: SHC; Mary Hill Joy, MPL MR; McIlwaine.

5. Napoleon Hill's $15,000 in gold: Mary Hill Joy (other accounts put the figure at $10,000).

6. Hill's wedding and return to "Sabine farm": HGFP: SHC; McIlwaine.

7. ". . . merchandising and not fighting . . .": MCA, June 18, 1911.

8. Yankee trading fleet: Hallum.

9. U. S. Grant and Josiah DeLoach: Mary Hill Joy; Grant; McFeely.

Mary Hill Joy gives an account of Grant's visit that differs somewhat with Grant's own published recollection of the event. Hill writes: "General Grant came to our home in Collierville [20 miles east of Memphis] during the war with his staff, and sat on our front porch and Mr. [Josiah] DeLoach [the Hills' step-father] handed him the morning paper and passed around refreshments, and my mother, 'ever on hospitable thoughts intent,' went out to order dinner for General Grant and his staff. While they were sitting there one of the servants came to my mother and told her that Confederates had crossed the river a few miles back of us, and my mother told Mr. DeLoach and Mr. DeLoach in turn told General Grant. General Grant immediately stood up and said, 'Well, gentlemen, this is very nice, but this is not going to Memphis.' So they jumped on their horses and rode away just as fast as they could."

In his *Personal Memoirs* Grant recalls that shortly before noon on June 23,

1862, he was riding toward Memphis when he spotted a "very comfortable-looking white-haired gentlemen" [DeLoach] seated on the porch of a house near the road. Telling his staff and escort to ride ahead, Grant stopped at the house and, "for an excuse, asked for a glass of water." Grant found DeLoach to be "very genial and communicative, [until] . . . a neighbor, a Dr. Smith . . . called and, on being presented to me, backed off the porch as if something had hit him."

Grant, noticing that DeLoach had stopped pressing him to stay for lunch, mounted his horse and rode on. A day or two later DeLoach made a point of looking Grant up in Memphis and apologizing for the apparent incivility, explaining that "the rebel General [John K.] Jackson [had been] in the neighborhood with a detachment of cavalry." DeLoach had been "sure that his neighbor knew it and would give information of my presence," Grant writes, "and he had felt restless until I got away."

Jackson's cavalry was indeed a few miles away when word reached them that Grant was visiting at the DeLoach house; but on arriving there and discovering that Grant's party had a 45-minute head start on them, Jackson decided to break off pursuit. Had Jackson "gone three-quarters of a mile further," writes Grant, "he would have found me with my party quietly resting under the shade of trees and without even arms in our hands with which to defend ourselves."

10. James Lusk Alcorn: Current; HGFP: SHC, letters.

Alcorn's daughters, Jessie and Gertrude, were frequently guests at parties given by the Napoleon Hills during the 1880s. At one party, Miss Gertrude appeared in a fairy-like costume of "white tulle brocaded in gold, pink skirt and slippers, golden wings, white satin traine, and Rhine stone ornaments." HGFP: SHC

11. "the Semmes came and Jefferson Davis": HGFP SHC, oral interview of Mary Wood Hill by Olivia Hill Grosvenor, circa 1920s.

12. Farrington's "most successful period": MCA, June 18, 1911.

13. Farrington and Beaumont: Keating (vol. 1); MCA, June 18, 1911; Fraser; MCA, April 23, 1933.

14. Chinese Labor Convention: Cribbs.

15. N. B. Forrest and Farrington: Lytle.

16. Farrington and the Memphis & Little Rock: UPNB board minutes, July 1875.

17. Farmers and Merchants Bank: Keating (vol. 1); Schweikart.

18. State Constitutional Convention of 1870: Thorogood.

19. Rawlings' "unspeakable fun": Rawlings

20. Greenlaw and the railroads: Coppock, (*Memphis Sketches*); UPNB board minutes, January 1874.

21. U and P stock subscription: UPNB board minutes, August 21, 1869.

22. Rawlings on Grover Cleveland: Rawlings.

23. Farrington appointed Postmaster: MCA, June 18, 1911.

2. "A Vast Pawn Shop"

On the crop-lien system: Clark; Coulter; ESH; Ballaugh, *The South in the Building of the Nation* (vol. VI); Woodward, (*Origins*); Wright.

On Memphis municipal finances, 1865–1875: Capers; Keating (vol. 2); Sigafoos; White; Wrenn.

On Yellow Fever: Dromgoole; Keating (vol. 1); LaPointe; McCullough; White; Wrenn.

1. "generously loaned . . .": Joseph G. Baldwin, *The Flush Times of Alabama and Mississippi.*

2. Jefferson Davis and other customers: UPNB, "Discount Tickler, 1875."

3. Bank as state depository: Farrington.

4. "Chicago of the lower West": Capers.

5. Planter to Napoleon Hill: HGFP: SHC.

6. Overdrafts: UPNB, board minutes, January 17, 1872.

7. Greenlaw's payments to editors of *Commercial Appeal:* Baker.

8. Greenlaw and Topp: Commonplace book of Elizabeth Vance Topp, RTP: RC BL.

9. Rift between directors and Farrington: Goyer, et al.

10. Run on Memphis banks: Baker, Farrington, Goyer et al., White.

3. The Bills Fall Due

On Memphis finances, 1870s: Capers; Clotfelter; Coulter; Sigafoos; Tucker ("Black Politics . . ."); Vance; Woodward (*Origins*).

On Yellow Fever: Baker; Carter; Defoe; Dromgoole; Keating (vol. 1); LaPointe; McCullough; White; Wrenn.

1. Forrest and Farrington: Lytle.

2. Topp's cotton claims: RTP: BL RC.

   Topp came out of the war a poor man. Despite his lobbying in Washington and Richmond, both sides eventually turned against him. In the fall of 1863, his neighbors in Bolivar County, Mississippi, enraged by his pro-Union sentiments, torched the cotton and some buildings on his plantation there. Then, in January 1864 and again in April, General W. T. Sherman seized large quantities of cotton that Topp was attempting to take north. After the war Topp "owed enormous debts," wrote his wife Elizabeth. "He said he would never walk the streets of Memphis while those were staring him in the face."

   Topp had to borrow money from his brother-in-law, William Vance, in order to leave Memphis during the cholera epidemic of 1873, by which time he was broken in more ways than financial. As Elizabeth Topp recalled: "The best lawyers in the country were employed by Mr. T—and they believed in his rights, but the courts decided the case [cotton claims] against him. He had no money to continue the suit. He might have carried it to Washington. I do not know why he did not except that his spirit was broken, his health had failed, and other projects filled his mind, which he thought would supersede all his old claims."

   In the winter of 1875–1876, Topp travelled across Florida, from Jacksonville to Tampa, making speeches in which he advocated that Congress be petitioned to appropriate large sums for the construction of "an immense industrial school and to develop the state with a system of railroads." On returning there was, Elizabeth wrote, "the seal of death on his face." Topp died later in 1876; his body was kept in the receiving vault at Elmwood Cemetery for several months, till the money for his burial was raised. RTP: RC BL

3. Directors' disagreement with Farrington: Goyer et al.

4. The board minutes do not tell who voted for whom, but in all probability Hill, Williamson, Bruce, Vaccaro, Treadwell and Galbreath voted for Goyer, while Ensley, Church, and Rawlings voted for Farrington. The number of directors had fallen from fifteen to thirteen, and two of them, Greenlaw and James Wilkins, were absent.

5. All words of Farrington are taken from his "Address to the Stockholders of the Union and Planters Bank of Memphis," unless otherwise noted.

6. Niles' words on Farrington: Tennessee Supreme Court case files, Farrington vs. Gayoso Hotel Company et al (filed July 1895 (TSLA). It should be noted, too, that Farrington's management of Robertson Topp's estate came in for severe criticism from Topp's widow, Elizabeth (RTP: RC BL).

7. All quotations from the directors' printed reply are taken from Goyer et al.

8. Other noteworthy loans were made to the City Board of Education ($900),

James L. Alcorn ($4,635), Memphis Gas Company ($68,000), Elmwood Cemetery ($6,600), Mississippi Tennessee Railroad Company ($22,651), A. Schwab ($10,000), and John Overton, Jr. ($2,204): (UPNB).

4. After the Yellow Fever

On Napoleon Hill: Clotfelter; HGFP: SHC; Charles Niles Grosvenor III to the author, May 4, 1989; Holden; Joy; McIlwaine; MCA, November 2, 1909; Tennessee State Supreme Court case files: Bank of Louisville vs. Hill, Fontaine Company, 1897 (TSLA); Hill vs. Crenshaw, 1912 (TSLA); Hill, Fontaine, Read vs. Selden Brick Company (TSLA).

On Memphis banks, 1880–1897: Coppock ("Looking at Banking"); Keating (vol. 1); Morrison; Tennessee State Supreme Court case file, Farrington vs. Gayoso Hotel Company (TSLA); UPNB board minutes.

On the Panic of 1893 and depression: Baker; ESH; Greider; Redlich; Sigafoos; Woodward (*Origins*); Wright.

On the People's Protective Union and charter repeal in Memphis: Bristow; Clotfelter; Coulter (*South During Reconstruction*); Miller (*Memphis During the Progressive Era*), Rawlings; Sigafoos; Vance.

1. Memphis bank clearings, late 1880s: Morrison.

2. Frederick Cossitt, Robertson Topp, and Brown Brothers: unsigned letter of April 10, 1864, in Topp's highly distinctive (and almost illegible) handwriting.

   Topp does not identify the addressee by name, but the detailed account Topp provides of his efforts to influence Lincoln's cabinet and the precise instructions he gives the addressee on handling Federal officers and Treasury officials in the trans-Mississippi lead to the conclusion that Topp is writing to none other than an intimate partner in the cotton trade. One likely possibility is his brother-in-law, William L. Vance.

   Certainly, neither Topp nor the addressee would have cared to be identified as the writer or the recipient of this letter were it to have fallen into the wrong hands, including those of Confederate officials and military commanders or General Grant, General Sherman, and Secretary of State Edwin Stanton. (Extracts from the letter are reproduced in footnote 2 to Chapter 1.) RTP: RC BL.

3. Napoleon Hill's estate: Tennessee Supreme Court case file, Hill vs. Crenshaw, 1912 (TSLA); HGFP: SHC.

4. "Don't *stint* yourself": Napoleon Hill to Mary Wood Hill, August 9, 1885 (HGFP: SHC).

5. Napoleon Hill's bedroom suite: McIlwaine.

6. "Champagne flowed like water": *Merriwether's Weekly,* November 11, 1882 (cited in *WTHSP,* vol. 5, p. 47).

7. Treadwell's charges against Read: All quotations are taken from UPNB board minutes, August–October 1885.

8. Union and Planters' loans to State of Tennessee: On December 6, 1887, the bank agreed to lend the state $30,000, and on June 19, 1888, agreed to lend an additional $30,000. UPNB board minutes of December 6, 1887, and June 19, 1888.

9. Farrington's debts: Tennessee Supreme Court case file, Farrington vs. Gayoso Hotel Company, Continental National Bank, B. M. Estes, and Memphis Trust Company (TSLA). The words quoted are those of C. F. M. Niles, president of Continental Bank in 1894–1895.

5. MR. READ'S BANK

On Banking in Memphis, 1900–1915: Coppock ("Looking Back . . ."), Elliott & Company Auditors, "Banking Facilities—Compiled Statement of Condition of Memphis Banks at Close of Business December 31, 1907 (UPNB); Gray; MCA, "Scrip Issue . . .", March 6, 1933; Morrison; Prochnow; Redlich; Tindall.
On the development of trust companies in the South: Redlich; Ballaugh, *The South in the Building of the Nation* (vol. VI), Warren.

1. Read's words on banking are taken from "Letter of S. P. Read to Memphis Chapter American Institute of Banking," 1910 (UPNB).

2. The term "resources" was defined as the total value of loans and discounts, overdrafts, banking furniture and fixtures, stocks and bonds, banking house and real estate, cash and exchange.

3. Fitzhugh's combativeness: In 1904, during a trial in which Fitzhugh defended his client against a suit brought by Union and Planters, he repeatedly questioned the relevance of a case cited by the presiding judge. When he finally informed the judge that he was unaware that the case was an authority in the suit before them, the bank's counsel, Kenneth D. McKellar, cooly remarked: "No, but his honor is." (Tennessee Supreme Court Case Files, Hill et. al. vs. Selden Brick Construction Company, 1904) Fitzhugh also initiated several ouster suits that removed from office popularly elected Memphis officials, including Ed Crump.

4. "almost the first rule . . .": Miller (*Mr. Crump of Memphis*).

5. Riley C. Garner, interview with the author, March 16, 1989.

6. "A GENTLEMAN TO THE MANNER BORN"

On Beale Street: Biles, Coppock (*Memphis Sketches*), DuBois, Handy, Tucker
(*Lieutenant Lee of Beale Street*).

On Frank F. Hill: Eastman; HGFP: SHC; Hill Mansion Records (MSU MVC);
Frank M. Gilliland to Vance J. Alexander, June 10, 1933; C. N. Grosvenor III
to the author, May 4, 1989; House; James Lancaster, interview with the au-
thor, February 14, 1989; *Memphis Magazine,* September 1978; Mooney; *MPS,*
March 14, 1935, and March 15, 1935, and April 31, 1935; UPNB, *Story of a
Memphis Institution.*

On Memphis Banking and Commerce, 1915–1924: Allen (*Lords of Creation*);
Cohn; McIlwaine; Prochnow; Sigafoos; Tindall.

On Robert S. Polk: HGFP: SHC, Elizabeth Anderson Hill to Olivia Hill
Grosvenor, April 5, 1924; Papers of Frank Hayden, 1924–1928 (UPNB);
MCA, March–April 1924; MPS, March–April 1924.

On Progressivism in Memphis: Bridges; Corlew; ESC; McIlwaine; Miller (*Mr.
Crump*); Tindall; Woodward (*Origins*).

1. "Well, I do": Boyce.

2. Ashcroft to Crump: Miller (*Mr. Crump*).

3. "a gentleman to the manner born": Mooney.

4. Comptroller's criticism of loans: Mercantile National Bank board minutes,
September 1917 (UPNB).

5. In 1908 Memphis renamed its east-west thoroughfares—thus the change from
Madison Street to Madison Avenue. A great many other names were done
away with altogether; for instance, DeSoto became Third Street, and Shelby
became South Front. Whiskey Chute, the saloon-lined alley running between
Front and Main streets less than a block from Union and Planters was later
given the more staid name of Park Lane.

6. As with so much of the new business brought in during the Hill administration, the correspondent accounts were not always profitable. In a letter of September 24, 1926 to Frank Hayden, Gilmer Winston explained: "We entertained the country bankers visiting Memphis; took them to the theatre,
baseball games, etc., and cultivated them at all times. . . . Things [were] done
which made the cost of securing new business too high . . . such as furnishing country banks paper at 6% and doing things for them for which we paid
dearly in return." (UPNB).

7. "that particular territory": Gilmer Winston to Caldwell and Company, February 9, 1929 (UPNB).

7. The Proposition from Nashville

On Rogers Caldwell and Luke Lea: Rogers Caldwell and T. H. Alexander; Baker; Barker; Rogers Caldwell to Vance J. Alexander, August–September 1933, Alexander Papers (UPNB); Hull; James Lancaster, interview with the author, January 26, 1989; Manhattan Savings and Trust board minutes, April 1928–December 1931; McFerrin; *Men of Tennessee;* Moore; Taylor.

1. In January 1922 the board set President Hill's salary at $40,000, and those of his principal officers, Bob Polk and Gilmer Winston, at $22,000 and $19,000 respectively. Hayden had the president's salary reduced to $25,000, and those of his two principal officers, Gilmer Winston and John J. Heflin, were fixed at $12,000.

2. The property at 67 Madison was acquired in 1922 by the Security Building Corporation, headed by B. A. Bogy. Construction started not long after January 15, 1923, when Rogers Caldwell originated and underwrote mortgage bonds of $670,000 for the Security Corporation. When the building opened in the fall of 1923, it was known as the Cotton States Life Building, its main tenant being the Cotton States Life Insurance Company. Before the end of 1923, however, Rogers Caldwell bought Cotton States Life and moved the company to Nashville. Union and Planters then acquired the building, on May 6, 1924, from Fred Callahan of the Security Corporation.

3. After the Fraternal's demise, many of its former customers opened accounts at the bank's Main Street Branch. Among them were the Inter-Racial League, the Memphis *Triangle,* the United Brotherhood of Railway Workers, the Universal Life Insurance Company, and the Beale Street political leader George W. Lee. But the gain in business was short-lived; Beale Street was dying. In 1932 the bank would close its branch there.

8. Mr. Alec and the Colonel

On the RFC-Union Planters loan to the Bank of Commerce: Alexander to K. D. McKellar (July 3 and 5, 1933), to T. O. Vinton (April 19, 1933), to J. M. Gardenhire (February 2, 1934), to William F. Sheehan (August 11, 1934), to Edward H. Crump (September 12, 1934); Ed Crump to Alexander, January 9, 1934; G. T. Fitzhugh to Alexander, April 26, 1934 and June 11, 1934; K. D. McKellar to Jesse Jones, September 12, 1934; Jones; Kennedy; *Press-Scimitar,* January 25, 1933.

1. Luke Lea was convicted in North Carolina of conspiracy to defraud, served two years of his sentence, received a full pardon in 1937 and lived quietly until his death in 1945. Governor Henry Horton, after narrowly escaping an impeachment trial before the State Senate, served out the remainder of his term in office, then retired from public life.

   Rogers Clark Caldwell was indicted by grand juries in Tennessee, Kentucky, North Carolina, and Arkansas, but was acquitted on all counts. The State of Tennessee obtained a $4.354 million judgment against him in 1938, but he continued to live in Brentwood House, a mansion modeled after Andrew Jackson's Hermitage, until 1957. A few years before his death in 1968, Caldwell told a Nashville reporter: "Sometimes I'll wake up in the middle of the night and think of all that might have happened and I think, my God! I'm lucky the way it turned out."

2. Paul Davis and the Crump-McAlister coalition: A. V. Louthan to Vance Alexander, January 6, 10, and 24, 1933; A. V. Louthan, "Facts Relating to the 1932 State and National Democratic Campaign in Tennessee," manuscript (Alexander Papers, UPNB).

3. "Mr. Crump was always partial . . .": Riley C. Garner, interview with the author, March 16, 1989.

4. RFC prediction of banking panic in Memphis: Kennedy.

5. Kenneth D. McKellar to Jesse Jones, September 12, 1934.

6. The plan to downsize Union Planters: Gilmer Winston to Robert Neill, October 29, 1932.

7. The directors who went off the board were M. J. Anderson, Thomas C. Ashcroft, A. H. Egan, John J. Heflin, J. E. Holmes, J. W. Keyes, Robert E. Lee, W. J. Prescott, Wassell Randolph, S. Steinberg, and Leslie M. Stratton.

9. "SANE, CONSERVATIVE OPENINGS"

On Arthur McCain: *Finance,* May 15, 1952; MPS, April 1 and 11, 1952. Anecdotal material obtained by the author in interviews with Vance Alexander, Jr. (March 3, 1989), Olivia Sauls (February 24, 1989), Leslie Stratton III (January 25, 1989), Charles Rauscher (February 24, 1989), and Russell Wood (January 17, 1989).

1. "Mr. Alec knew how . . .": This statement was made by at least two retired officers during interviews with the author.

2. "fine old rundown institution": Alexander Papers (UPNB).

3. Bank Management Committee minutes, April 15, 1952.

4. "a new bull in the pasture": Alexander Papers (UPNB).

10. MARKING TIME

On John E. Brown and Ben Harrison: a great deal of material was obtained during interviews with Jack R. Bulliner, Leo Fristrom, Bob Johnson, Charles Rauscher, Olivia Sauls, James F. Springfield, Leslie Stratton III, Richard A. Trippeer, Jr., Jerry Wood, and Russell Wood.

1. "the leadership was unbelievable": J. Armistead Smith, interview with the author, February 23, 1989.

2. "We didn't need an organization chart": James F. Springfield, interview with the author, December 14, 1990.

3. As late as 1971, Union Planters was carrying $17 million in "substandard" loans related to the 100 North Main Building.

4. Cecil Humphreys: board minutes of February 1967; Sorrells.

11. "THE ROLLERCOASTER YEARS"

On C. H. and Jake Butcher: Chattanooga *Times,* May 29–31 and June 1–3, 1983; Daughtery, et al.; MCA, June 9, 1983; UPNB executive committee minutes, January 23, 1975. Interviews by the author with Benjamin W. Rawlins, Jr., June 6, 1991; Joe Rives, January 18, 1989; J. Armistead Smith, February 23, 1989; and Richard A. Trippeer, Jr., January 16, 1989.

On William M. Matthews, Jr.: *American Banker,* February 21, 1978; Daughtery, et al.; David Flaum, MCA, September 23 and 28, 1984; Matthews to Eliot Janeway, UPC annual report 1981; Lewis Nolan, MCA, April 3, 1984; Pepin; Bruce Sankey, MCA, January 31, 1975. Interviews by the author with Robert Colbert, Jr., February 21, 1989; James A. Cook, Jr., March 25 and 26, 1994; Bob Johnson, February 23, 1989; Benjamin W. Rawlins, Jr., January 5, 1989, June 6, 1991, and February 12, 1994; James F. Springfield, December 7 and 9, 1988; Timmons L. Treadwell III, February 23, 1989; Richard A. Trippeer, Jr., September 29, 1988 and January 16, 1989.

1. loan review: *Business Week,* October 27, 1975; Thomas A. Garrison, interview with the author, March 14, 1989; Pepin; Charles Rauscher, interview with the author, February 24, 1989.

2. "leverage to the hilt": James A. Gurley, in Pepin, p. 90.

3. Daughtery, et al., p. 5.

4. Ibid, p. 9.

5. Ibid, p. 10.

6. Union Planters Annual Report, 1973.

7. Richard A. Trippeer, Jr., interview with the author, September 29, 1988.

8. Pepin, p. 116.

9. Ibid, p. 109.

10. Union Planters Executive Committee Minutes, November 7, 1974.

11. Pepin, p. 122.

12. Ibid, p. 122.

13. Daughtery, et al., p. 11.

14. Ibid, p. 10.

15. Pepin, p. 126.

16. Morgan, Keegan & Company, "Union Planters Corporation," Sepember 11, 1981.

17. Union Planters Annual Report, 1981.

18. Lewis Nolan, "UP—'real right' or 'horribly wrong,' " MCA, April 3, 1984.

12. Striking A Balance

1. Benjamin W. Rawlins, Jr., interview with the author, February 12, 1994.

2. Union Planters Annual Report, 1984.

3. J. Armistead Smith, interview with the author, February 23, 1989.

4. Bruce Hansen, "New UP President Plots Course as Acquisitions Build Assets," *Memphis Business Journal,* May 4–8, 1992.

5. Union Planters Annual Report, 1989.

6. Benjamin W. Rawlins, Jr., interview with the author, June 6, 1991 and February 12, 1994.

7. Remarks of Stieven and Coffey are cited in Union Planters Annual Report, 1989.

8. Union Planters Annual Report, 1990, p. 10.

9. Union Planters Annual Report, 1993, p. 22.

10. Nancy Pellegrino, "Union Planters Corporation," *BankWatch,* December 29, 1993.

11. Alan F. Morel, "Union Planters Corporation," Hilliard Lyons, February 4, 1994.

Bibliography

Abernathy, Thomas P. "The Early Development of Commerce and Banking in Tennessee." *Mississippi Valley Historical Review* XIV (1929).

Agee, James and Walker Evans. *Let Us Now Praise Famous Men.* Boston: Houghton Mifflin, 1941.

Alexander, Vance J. "Is There a Lesson in Cotton Financing?" *The Burroughs Clearing House,* March 1937.

————. Papers, 1933–1958. Collection of Union Planters National Bank Memphis, Tennessee.

Allen, Frederick Lewis. *The Lords of Creation.* London: Hamish Hamilton, 1935.

————. *Only Yesterday; An Informal History of the 1920s.* New York: Harper and Row, 1931.

American Banker. "Hard-Driving Matthews Turns Profit at Shaken Union Planters." February 21, 1978.

Anderson, George L. "The South and Problems of Post-Civil War Finance." *Journal of Southern History* IX (1943).

Baedeker's United States 1893: A Handbook for Travellers. New York, 1893.

Baker, Thomas H. *The Memphis Commercial Appeal.* Baton Rouge: Louisiana State University Press, 1971.

Baldwin, Joseph G. *The Flush Times of Alabama and Mississippi.* New York: Appleton, 1853 (LSU reprint, 1987).

Ballaugh, James C. ed. *The South in the Building of the Nation,* vol. VI. Richmond: Southern Publications Society, 1909.

Barker, George. "The Rise and Fall of Rogers Caldwell." *Nashville Tennessean,* Sunday magazine supplements of October 20, 27, and November 3, 1963.

Biles, Roger. *Memphis in the Great Depression.* Knoxville: University of Tennessee Press, 1986.

Blotner, Joseph. *Faulkner: A Biography.* 2 vols. New York: Random House, 1974.

Bridges, Lamar Whitlow. "Editor Mooney Versus Boss Crump." *West Tennessee Historical Society Papers* 20 (1966).

Bristow, Eugene K. "From Temple to Barn: The Greenlaw Opera House in Memphis, 1860–1880." *West Tennessee Historical Society Papers* 21 (1967).

Brooks, John. "A Corner in Piggly Wiggly." *New Yorker,* June 6, 1959.

Caldwell, Rogers Clark and T. H. Alexander. "A Rich Man's Son Earns His Own Success." *The New South,* March 1927.

Capers, Gerald M., Jr. *The Biography of A River Town; Memphis: Its Heroic Age.* New Orleans: by the author, 1966.

―――. "Satrapy of a Benevolent Despot." In Robert S. Allen, ed. *Our Fair City.* New York: Vanguard Press, 1947.

―――. "Yellow Fever in Memphis in the 1870s." *Mississippi Valley Historical Review* (24) 1937–38.

Carter, William C., ed. *Conversations with Shelby Foote.* Jackson: University Press of Mississippi, 1989.

Commercial and Statistical Review of the City of Memphis, Tennessee. Memphis: Reilly & Thomas, 1883.

Compton, Eric N. *Inside Commercial Banking.* New York: John Wiley & Sons, 1980.

Cash, Wilbur J. *The Mind of the South.* New York: Random House, 1941.

Clark, Thomas D. "The Furnishing and Supply System in Southern Agriculture since 1865." *Journal of Southern History* XII (1946).

Clotfelter, Charles. "Memphis Business Leadership and the Politics of Fiscal Crisis." *West Tennessee Historical Society Papers* 27 (1973).

Cohn, David L. *The Life and Times of King Cotton.* New York: Oxford University Press, 1956.

Coppock, Paul R. "Looking Back at Banking." *Planters Profiles* September 1973.

―――. *Memphis Memoirs.* Memphis: Memphis State University Press, 1980.

―――. *Memphis Sketches.* Memphis: Friends of the Memphis and Shelby County Libraries, 1976.

―――. *Paul R. Coppock's MidSouth.* Memphis: West Tennessee Historical Society, 1985.

Corlew, Robert E. *Tennessee: A Short History.* Knoxville: University of Tennessee Press, 1981.

―――, John Longwith, et al. *Tennessee: The Volunteer State.* Windsor Publications, 1989.

Coulter, E. Merton. "Commercial Intercourse with the Confederacy in the Mississippi Valley, 1861–1865." *The Mississippi Valley Historical Review,* March 1919.

―――. *The South During Reconstruction, 1865–1877.* Baton Rouge: LSU Press, 1947.

Cribbs, Lennie Austin. "The Memphis Chinese Labor Convention." *West Tennessee Historical Society Papers* 37 (1983).

Current, Richard Nelson. *Those Terrible Carpetbaggers.* New York: Oxford University Press, 1988.

Daughtrey, Larry et al. "Borrowed Money, Borrowed Time: The Fall of the House of Butcher." *Nashville Tennessean,* October 24–November 12, 1983.

Defoe, Daniel. *A Journal of the Plague Year.* London: 1722; reprint edition, New York: Penguin, 1986.

Dodge, Bertha S. *Cotton: The Plant That Would Be King.* Austin, University of Texas Press, 1984.

Dromgoole, J. P. *Yellow Fever Heroes, Honors, and Horrors of 1878.* Louisville: J. P. Morton and Company, 1879.

DuBois, W. E. B. "Black Banks and White in Memphis." *Crisis* 35 (May 1928).

Eastman, R. *Memphians in the Limelight.* Memphis: undated; circa 1910.

Eller, Ronald D. *Miners, Millhands, and Mountaineers: Industrialization of the Appalachian South, 1880–1930.* Knoxville: University of Tennessee Press, 1982.

Evans, Walker. *Photographs for the Farm Security Administration 1935–1938.* New York: De Capo Press, 1973.

Fakes, T. J. "Steamer 'Josie Harry' Queen of the White River Packets." Woodruff County [Arkansas] Historical Society publication of *Rivers and Roads and Points in Between,* vol. X: 3 (Summer 1982).

Farrington, William M. "Address to the Stockholders of the Union and Planters Bank of Memphis." Memphis: privately printed, September 26, 1874.

Federal Writers' Project. *Arkansas: A Guide to the State.* Hastings House, 1941.

———. *Mississippi: A Guide to the Magnolia State.* New York: Viking Press, 1938.

———. *Tennessee: A Guide to the State.* New York: Viking Press, 1939.

Foote, Shelby. *The Civil War: A Narrative; Red River to Appomattox.* New York: Random House, 1974.

Fraser, Walter J., Jr. "Lucien Bonaparte Eaton: Politics and the Memphis *Post* 1867–1869." *West Tennessee Historical Society Papers* 20 (1966).

Galbraith, John Kenneth. *The Great Crash of 1929.* Boston: Houghton Mifflin Company, 1954.

Garraty, John A. *The Great Depression.* New York: Doubleday, 1987.

Goyer, C. W. et al. "To the Stockholders of the Union Planters' Bank." *Daily Memphis Avalanche,* October 8, 1874.

Graham, Jeanne. "Kenneth McKellar's 1934 Campaign: Issues and Events." *West Tennessee Historical Society Papers* 18, 1964.

Grant, Ulysses Simpson. *Personal Memoirs.* 1885 (De Capo reprint, 1986).

Gray, Warren P. "The Development of Banking in Tennessee." Master's thesis, Stonier Graduate School of Banking, 1948.

Greider, William. "The Annals of Finance." *New Yorker,* November 9, 16, and 23, 1987.

Hallum, John. *Diary of an Old Lawyer.* Nashville, 1895.

Hammond, Bray. *Banks and Politics in America from the Revolution to the Civil War.* London: Oxford University Press, 1957.

Handy, William C. *Father of the Blues: An Autobiography.* New York: Macmillan, 1941.

Harkins, John E. *Metropolis of the American Nile: Memphis and Shelby County.* California: Windsor Publications, 1982.

Heavrin, Charles A. *Boxes, Baskets and Boards: A History of the Anderson-Tully Company.* Memphis: Memphis State University Press, 1981.

Henry, Robert Selph. *First With the Most Forrest.* Wilmington, North Carolina: Broadfoot Publishing Company, 1987.

Hill and Grosvenor Family Papers, 1860–1952. Manuscript Department, University of North Carolina Library at Chapel Hill.

Hill Mansion Records. Mississippi Valley Collection, Memphis State University.

Holden, John A., ed. "Journey of A Confederate Mother." *West Tennessee Historical Society Papers* 19 (1965).

Holmes, William F. *The White Chief: James Kimble Vardaman.* Baton Rouge: LSU Press, 1970.

House, Boyce. "Memphis Memories of 50 Years Ago." *WTHSP* 14 (1960).

House, Emmett J. Papers, 1950–1959. Collection of Union Planters National Bank, Memphis.

Hull, Cordell. *Memoirs.* 2 vols. New York: Macmillan, 1948.

Johnson, A. B. *A Treatise On Banking.* Utica, New York: Seward and Thurber, 1850.

Jones, Buck and Ann Hammock. "Bradford's Banking Briefs: A Perspective on the South's Leading Banking Organizations." Nashville: J. C. Bradford & Company, 1980.

Jones, Jesse Holman and Edward Angly. *Fifty Billion Dollars: My Thirteen Years With the RFC (1932–1945).* New York: Macmillan, 1951.

Joy, Mary Hill. "Genealogy of the Hill Family and Personal Recollections of Mrs. Mary Francis Hill Joy." Manuscript, Memphis Public Library.

Keating, John M. *History of the City of Memphis and Shelby County, Tennessee.* 2 vols. (Vol. 2 by O. F. Vedder). Syracuse, New York: D. Mason & Co., 1888.

Kennedy, Susan Estabrook. *The Banking Crisis of 1933.* Lexington, Kentucky: University of Kentucky Press, 1973.

Kross, Herman E., ed. *Documentary History of Banking and Currency in the United States.* 4 vols. New York: Chelsea House, 1969.

Lanier, Robert A. *Memphis in the Twenties: The Second Term of Mayor Rowlett Paine 1924–1928.* Memphis, Zenda Press, 1979.

LaPointe, Patricia: *From Saddlebags to Science: A Century of Health Care in Memphis, 1830 to 1930.* Memphis, 1984.

Leuchtenburg, William E. *The Perils of Prosperity, 1914–1932.* Chicago: University of Chicago Press, 1958.

Longinotti, Edward F. Papers, 1950–1959. Collection of Union Planters National Bank, Memphis.

———. "Small Loan Banking." *The Burroughs Clearing House,* May 1939.

Longwith, John. *Building to Last: The Story of the American National Bank and Trust Company.* Chattanooga: American National Bank, 1984.

Lumpkin, J. W. "Memphis and Its Manufacturing Advantages." *DeBow's Review,* X: 525–29.

Lyons, Sam B. "Another Growth Year for Union Planters." *Finance,* January 15, 1958.

Lytle, Andrew. *Bedford Forrest and His Critter Company.* New York: McDowell, Oblensky, 1960.

Manhattan Savings Bank & Trust Company. Board Minutes, 1885–1928.

McCullough, David. *The Path Between the Seas: The Creation of the Panama Canal 1870–1914.* New York: Simon & Schuster, 1977.

McElvaine, Robert S. *The Great Depression: America, 1929–1941.* New York: Times Books, 1984.

McFeely, William S. *Grant: A Biography.* New York: W. W. Norton, 1981.

McFerrin, John Berry. *Caldwell and Company: A Southern Financial Empire.* Chapel Hill: University of North Carolina Press, 1939.

McIlwaine, Shields. *Memphis Down in Dixie.* New York: Dutton, 1948.

McKelvey, Rosemary. "Union Planters National is 100 Years Old!" *Mid-Continent Banker,* August 1969.

McPherson, James M. *Battle Cry of Freedom: The Civil War Era.* New York: Oxford University Press, 1988.

Memphis As She Is. Memphis: Memphis Historical and Descriptive Publishing Company, 1887.

Memphis Chamber of Commerce Journal, January 1919–December 1923.

Memphis in Pictures: The Thirties. Memphis: Don Lancaster Company, 1985.

Memphis Social Register and Directory 1935. Memphis, 1935.

Men of Memphis. Undated, no publisher named. Memphis Public Library.

Mercantile National Bank. Board Minutes, 1914–1918.

Miller, William D. "The Browning-Crump Battle: The Crump Side." *East Tennessee Historical Society's Publications* 37 (1965).

———. *Memphis During the Progressive Era.* Memphis: Memphis State University Press, 1957.

———. *Mr. Crump of Memphis.* Baton Rouge: LSU Press, 1964.

Mooney, C. P. J., ed. *The MidSouth and Its Builders; Being the Story of the Development and a Forecast of the Future of the Richest Agricultural Region in the World.* Memphis: MidSouth Biographical and Historical Association, 1920.

Moore, John Trotwood, and Austin P. Foster. *Tennessee: The Volunteer State, 1769–1923.* Chicago: S. J. Clarke Publishing Company, 1923.

Moore, D. D. *Men of the South: A Work for the Newspaper Reference Library.* New Orleans: Southern Biographical Association, 1922.

Morris, Willie. "Faulkner's Mississippi." *National Geographic,* February 1989.

Morrison, Andrew. *Memphis, Tennessee, The Bluff City.* St. Louis: George W. Engelhardt, 1892.

Morgan, Keegan & Company. "Union Planters Corporation." Memphis: Morgan, Keegan, September 11, 1981.

Myers, Margaret G. *A Financial History of the United States* New York: Columbia University Press, 1970.

National City Bank (Memphis). Board Minutes, 1918–1930. Collection of Union Planters National Bank, Memphis.

Naipual, V. S. *A Turn in the South.* New York: Alfred A. Knopf, 1989.

Parks, Joseph H. "A Confederate Trade Center Under Federal Occupation: Memphis, 1862–1865." *Journal of Southern History* 7 (August 1941).

Pepin, John J. *The Turnaround.* Oklahoma City: Western Heritage Books, 1980.

Percy, William Alexander. *Lanterns on the Levee: Recollections of a Planter's Son.* New York: Alfred A. Knopf, 1941 (LSU Press reprint, 1988).

Prochnow, Herbert V., ed. *The Federal Reserve System*. New York: Harper & Brothers, 1960.

Rawlings, J. J. *Miscellaneous Writings and Reminiscences*. Memphis: 1895.

Read, Samuel P. "Letter of S. P. Read to Memphis Chapter American Institute of Banking." Memphis: S. C. Toof & Co., 1910. Collection of Union Planters National Bank.

Redlich, Fritz. *The Molding of American Banking*. New York: Johnson Reprint Corporation, 1957.

Reese, Issac. "Memphis as a Future Iron and Steel Center." *Memphis Chamber of Commerce Journal*. November 1919.

Roller, David C. and Robert W. Twyman, eds. *The Encyclopedia of Southern History*. Baton Rouge: Louisiana State University Press, 1979.

Roper, James E., ed. *Chronicles of the Farmers' and Merchants' Bank of Memphis (1832–1847) by Jesse the 'Scribe.'* Memphis: Southwestern, Burrow Library Monograph number 4, 1960.

Schlesinger, Arthur M., Jr. *The Age of Roosevelt: The Coming of the New Deal*. Boston: Houghton Mifflin, 1959.

Schuler, Stanley. *Mississippi Valley Architecture: Houses of the Lower Mississippi Valley*. Exton, PA: Schiffer Publishing Ltd., 1984.

Schweikart, Larry. *Banking in the American South from the Age of Jackson to Reconstruction*. Baton Rouge: LSU Press, 1987.

Sharp, James A. "The Entrance of the Farmers' Alliance into Tennessee Politics." *East Tennessee Historical Society's Publications*, 9 (1937).

Sherman, William T. *Memoirs*. New York: Appleton, 1875.

Sigafoos, Robert A. *Cotton Row to Beale Street: A Business History of Memphis*. Memphis: Memphis State University Press, 1979.

Singer, Mark. *Funny Money*. New York: Alfred A. Knopf, 1985.

Sorrells, William. *The Exciting Years: The Cecil C. Humphreys Presidency of MSU 1960–1972*. Memphis: Memphis State University Press, 1987.

Studenski, Paul and Herman E. Kross. *Financial History of the United States*. New York: McGraw-Hill, 1963.

Taylor, Peter. *A Summons to Memphis*. New York: Knopf, 1986.

Tennessee Supreme Court Case Files. Farrington vs. Gayoso Hotel Company, Continental National Bank, B. M. Estes, and Memphis Trust Company, 1897 (Tennessee State Library and Archives).

———. Napoleon Hill, Noland Fontaine, S. P. Read vs. Selden Brick Construction Company and National Surety Company, 1904 (Tennessee State Library and Archives).

Terkel, Studs. *Hard Times: An Oral History of the Great Depression.* New York: Simon & Schuster, 1978.

Terrill, Tom E. and Jerold Hirsch. *Such As Us: Southern Voices of the Thirties.* Chapel Hill: University of North Carolina Press, 1978.

Thorogood, James E. *A Financial History of Tennessee Since 1870.* Sewanee, Tennessee, 1949.

Tindall, George B. *The Emergence of the New South, 1913–1945.* Baton Rouge: LSU Press, 1967.

Topp, Robertson. Papers. RC BL.

Trollope, Fanny. *Domestic Manners of the Americans.* London, 1832.

Tucker, David M. "Black Politics in Memphis, 1865–1878." *West Tennessee Historical Society Papers* 26 (1972).

————. *Lieutenant Lee of Beale Street.* Nashville: Vanderbilt University Press, 1971.

————. *Memphis Since Crump: Bossism, Blacks, and Civic Reformers 1848–1968.* Knoxville: University of Tennessee Press, 1980.

Twain, Mark. *Life on the Mississippi.* 1883.

————. and Charles Dudley Warner. *The Gilded Age.* 1873.

Union Planters National Bank. Annual Reports, 1956–1993.

————. Board Minutes, 1869–1892, 1935–1988.

————. Executive Committee Minutes, 1933–1988.

————. Payroll Ledgers, 1919–1969.

————. *The Story of a Memphis Institution, 1869–1919.* Memphis: Union & Planters Bank and Trust Company (commemorative history), 1919.

Walking Through Old Memphis. Memphis: Memphis Heritage Press, 1981.

Warner, Charles Dudley. "Studies of the Great West: Memphis and Little Rock." *Harper's New Monthly Magazine* LXXVII (1889).

Warren, Robert Penn. *The Legacy of the Civil War.* Cambridge University Press, 1961.

————. *Jefferson Davis Gets His Citizenship Back.* University Press of Kentucky, 1980.

White, Mimi. "Yellow Fever." Supplement to Memphis *Commercial Appeal,* October 31, 1978.

Who's Who in Tennessee. Memphis: Paul and Douglas Company, 1911.

Wilson, Charles Reagan and William Ferris, eds. *Encyclopedia of Southern Culture.* Chapel Hill: University of North Carolina Press, 1989.

Winston, Gilmer. Papers, 1932–1938. Collection of Union Planters National Bank, Memphis.

Woodward, C. Vann. *Reunion and Reaction: The Compromise of 1877 and the End of Reconstruction.* Boston: Little, Brown and Company, 1951.

———. *Origins of the New South: 1877–1913.* Louisiana State University Press, 1951.

———. *Thinking Back: The Perils of Writing History.* LSU Press, 1986.

Wrenn, Lynette Boney. "The Impact of Yellow Fever on Memphis: A Reappraisal." *West Tennessee Historical Society Papers* 41 (1987).

Wright, Gavin. *Old South, New South: Revolutions in the Southern Economy Since the Civil War.* New York: Basic Books, 1986.

Wyatt-Brown, Bertram. *Southern Honor: Ethics and Behavior in the Old South.* Oxford: Oxford University Press, 1982.

Young, J. P. *Standard History of Memphis, Tennessee: From A Study of the Original Sources.* Knoxville: H. W. Crew & Co., 1912 (1974 *West Tennessee Historical Society Papers* reprint).

Appendix A

CHRONOLOGY

1860   DeSoto Insurance & Trust Company (incorporated March 1858),
       located at 42 Madison, is managed by William Farrington, C. B.
       Church, W. B. Galbreath, C. W. Goyer, W. B. Greenlaw, and J. J.
       Rawlings.

1869   (February 12): William Farrington secures legislation enabling DeSoto
       Insurance & Trust to convert from the life insurance to the banking
       business.

       (June 1): Stockholders vote to convert DeSoto into a banking firm to
       be named Union and Planters Bank of Memphis. Outstanding fire
       risks are re-insured, marine policies are cancelled.

       (August 9): Authorized stock of $300,000 is said to be fully
       subscribed; board of Union and Planters authorizes an additional
       offering up to total of $600,000.

       (August 21): Fifteen directors are elected: William M. Farrington, J. J.
       Rawlings, Charles B. Church, John Johnson, Charles Wesley Goyer,
       William B. Greenlaw, William B. Galbreath, Napoleon Hill,
       Antonio Vaccaro, Joseph Bruce, Zeno N. Estes, M. L. Meacham,
       William A. Williamson, James A. Rogers, and Nathan Adams. In
       addition to the directors there are 13 other stockholders. An
       advertisement announces that Union and Planters will "open a
       general banking business" on September 1, and "until completion of
       their new building at 11 Madison [now 73 Madison] offices will be
       at 16 Madison [now 80 Madison]." Board sets total amount of
       authorized capital at $1 million; subscriptions for $671,300 are
       received by end of August. William Farrington is elected president,
       Samuel P. Read cashier, and William Williamson vice-president.

       (September 1): Union and Planters opens with a full-time staff of the
       cashier, a teller, and two bookkeepers.

       (October 26): Takes over the assets and accounts of People's Bank.

1870   (January 31): Moves into building at 11 Madison.

       (February 16): Becomes the West Tennessee depository for state of
       Tennessee.

(April): Discounts and notes of $339,648; cash on hand of $218,229.30. Dividends of 6 percent declared.

1871   (October 25): As Memphis municipal debt soars, the directors vote to sell all the bank's Memphis bonds.

1872   (January): Audit committee finds overdrafts "unusually large" at $263,009.25.

1873   (February): Farrington to defend stockholders against taxes assessed on stock by city, county and state.

(September 14): Yellow fever declared epidemic in Memphis; thousands flee the town.

(September 18): Financial Panic of 1873 boils up as New York banking house of Jay Cooke, over-extended by railroad financing, closes its door. By year end, 55 railroads in default and their financing banks in trouble.

(September 21): New York banking firm of P. M. Meyers Company suspends payment, owing Union and Planters $51,977.31.

(September 25): Special meeting held to decide whether to suspend operations because of the "terrible panic now prevailing here and elsewhere." Board votes to continue "paying currency to all whom it was due."

1874   (January 14): Board extends thanks to employees and officers for their steadfastness during the epidemic; awards them cash bonuses. The board removes Farrington from the presidency, replacing him with C. W. Goyer.

(January 21): Audit committee reports discounts and notes of $708,406.63 ($111,000 of which are past due), and $74,753 in overdrafts. Board votes to limit and control lending to directors.

1875   (January 30): Capital stock reduced from $1 million to $600,000.

(July 5): Profit of $33,436 for first six months of year.

1876   (May): Mayor Flippin applies for loan to city; board declines the loan.

1878   (August 14): Board meets as yellow fever sweeps the city. More than half the population flees. Of some 20,000 remaining, 14,000 are black or Irish. 17,000 are stricken and by October, when first frost ends the epidemic, 75 percent are dead.

(December 11): A Resolutions Committee presents thanks to employees and officers. Board votes bonus of two months double salary to president Goyer, cashier Read, and all employees "who remained at their posts" during the epidemic. One teller, Louis Czapski, died of the fever; his bonus goes to his wife and children.

(December 25): Stockholders present Read with a $500, stem-winding Jurgensen Chronometer in appreciation of his service during the epidemic.

1879   Deep in debt, Memphis gives up its city charter, becoming a taxing district of the state.

1880   (July): profit of $37,331 for the first half of year.

1881   (January): loans and discounts total $1.09 million; cash on hand is $265,222; deposits amount to $857,399. Past due notes down to $22,305.98.

(February 22): President Goyer dies. Board meets later in the day and elects Williamson president. He declines to serve; A. C. Treadwell is then elected president. Samuel Read is named to Goyer's vacant seat on board.

1882   (January 2): Deposits of $850,627; loans of $1.3 million.

1883   (January): Deposits total $1.09 million; overdrafts of $11,268. Board consists of Edmond M. Apperson, Joseph Bruce, Enoch Ensley, J. F. Frank, W. B. Galbreath, Napoleon Hill, Henry B. Howell, M. P. Jarnigan, T. J. Latham, A. N. McKay, Samuel Read, A. C. Treadwell, Antonio Vaccaro, William Williamson.

1885   (January): loans of $1.24 million; deposits of $820,466.

(June 11): Directors agree to take up to $25,000 of Taxing District bonds at par, in order to help retire the major portion of old municipal debt.

(August 8–October 7): President Treadwell charges Cashier Read with "irregularities." A committee named to investigate the charge exonerates Read. Treadwell resigns, as do Directors Frank and Galbreath. On Read's nomination, Napoleon Hill is elected president.

1887   (December 6): After meeting with Governor, President Hill proposes, and board agrees, to lend the state $30,000 to meet bond interest due in January 1888.

1888   (July 8): By-laws amended to read: "No Cashier, Teller, Bookkeeper or clerk in the employ of this Bank shall keep an account with it."

1889   (January 7): Directors note a "stagnation" in economic activity.

(April): President Hill leaves on an extended trip to Mexico and California.

1892   (July 5): As local economy worsens, directors cut the dividend to 5 percent.

1893   (May): Financial Panic, with effects continuing until Spanish American War. Within 2 years, almost one-quarter of total railroad capitalization is in bankruptcy; wheat and cotton prices collapse; the unemployed total three million, and Coxey's Army marches on Washington. A consortium of New York bankers headed by J. P. Morgan helps President Cleveland maintain the enthreatened gold standard.

1894   (November): A stroke impairs President Hill. Two years later another stroke partially paralyzes him.

1897   (January): S. P. Read replaces Hill as president.

1900   Deposits of $1.33 million; eight employees.

1906   (May 1) Acquires the Tennessee Trust Company, bringing deposits to just under $5 million. Name changed to Union and Planters Bank & Trust Company. Moves into the 15-story building of Tennessee Trust at 77-79 Madison [now 81 Madison] The acquisition brings to the board seven new directors, including Gus T. Fitzhugh, B. L. Mallory, Frank M. Norfleet, John Pepper, and Henry Winkelman.

1907   Deposits of $4.77 million place it second among Memphis banks, behind the Bank of Commerce with $5.95 million. Third in deposits is First National, with $2.89 million.

1909   (November): Napoleon Hill dies.

1911   (November): William Farrington dies.

1914   Outbreak of war in Europe disturbs financial and cotton markets.

1915   (February): Samuel Read dies.

         (March 11): Frank Hill is elected to succeed Read as president. Deposits of $5 million; resources of $7.4 million.

1917   (November): Joins the Federal Reserve System; said to be one of the first state-chartered banks in Tennessee to do so.

1918   (February 16): Buys Mercantile National Bank, located at 109 Madison.

1919   Memphis marks its 100th birthday, Union and Planters its 50th. With a population of some 162,000, Memphis is the fifth largest city in the South, and Union and Planters' deposits of $19.85 million make it the largest bank in Memphis. 167 employees. Board consists of Thomas C. Ashcroft, Harry Cohn, Noland Fontaine, Jr., Guston T. Fitzhugh, W. E. Gage, Frank Hill, J. F. Holst, Thomas H. Jackson, R. L. Jordan, Samuel Leatherman, B. Lee Mallory, John D. Martin, J. W. McClure, J. M. McCormack, John D. McDowell, Frank

Norfleet, Jesse Norfleet, Robert Polk, Leslie M. Stratton, John T. Walsh, Henry T. Winkelman, and Gilmer Winston.

1922   Main Street branch opens at Main and Beale.

1923   (June): Buys North Memphis Savings Bank (established in 1904 by John and Anthony Walsh) and converts it into a branch.

1924   (March): An audit reveals that Robert Polk, a top executive, has absconded with large sums. These and other losses impair the bank's capital structure.

(April): Frank Hayden of Guaranty Bank and Trust Company replaces Frank Hill as president, with Union and Planters acquiring the Guaranty.

(August): Main office moved to the 12-story building at southeast corner of Front and Madison.

(September): Capital stock is cut in half, dividend is suspended.

1926   Franklin Savings branch, 109 Madison, closes.

1927   (January 27): Pays first dividend since 1924.

(August): An installment lending department, said to be one of the first in the South, opens under the direction of Vice-president Edward Longinotti at the North Memphis branch.

1928   (July 7): A run breaks out at the bank and at the North Memphis branch.

(December): News article reports that Rogers Caldwell, Luke Lea, and other investors will reorganize the bank, injecting large sums of capital.

1929   (February 28): Stockholders vote to sell about 69% of total shares to Rogers Caldwell and others.

(March): Applies for a national banking charter.

(April): Rogers Caldwell, Luke Lea, and other major stockholders sign, at the request of U.S. Comptroller of the Currency, a letter agreeing not to remove any assets from the bank.

(July 9): Receives national banking charter, in name of Union Planters National Bank and Trust Company.

(October 7): William White elected president, while Hayden is named chairman of board.

(December 19): Hayden resigns; White remains as president and chairman of board, which is made up of M. J. Anderson, Thomas Ashcroft, Fred Bianchi, Robert Bruce, James E. Caldwell, Meredith

Caldwell, Rogers Caldwell, A. H. Egan, John J. Heflin, J. E. Holmes, J. W. Keyes, Robert E. Lee, B. L. Mallory, Joseph Maury, J. M. McCormack, Lytle McKee, Hirsch Morris, William Orgill, Edward Potter, Jr., W. J. Prescott, John A. Reichman, Lant Salsbury, S. Steinberg, Leslie Stratton, Hillsman Taylor, Edward Tefft, T. H. Tutwiler, Edwin Warner, William White, Henry Winkelman, and Gilmer Winston.

1930   (July 27): White resigns and Edward P. Peacock is named president. Capital, surplus and undistributed profits total $8.34 million; deposits of $22.56 million.

(November) Caldwell and Company fails. American National of Nashville acquires a large interest in Union Planters.

1932   (January 14): Gilmer Winston succeeds Peacock as president. The Great Depression deepens.

1933   (March): A run depletes cash at the Bank of Commerce; Union Planters participates in an RFC loan enabling Bank of Commerce to remain open. President Roosevelt declares a nationwide banking moratorium.

(March 11): Assumes the deposit liabilities of the Manhattan branch.

(April 8): Vance J. Alexander elected president in a reorganization plan designed by J. Walter Canada and others. A substantially new board is elected.

(June 30): Reported deposits of $26.14 million.

(November 29): Reported deposits of $33.62 million.

1935   Qualifies for federal deposit insurance.

1936   Working control returns to stockholders in Memphis.

1937   (March): Opens a $150,000 addition to main office, one of the first such building programs in Memphis since the Depression's onset.

1939   (May): Gilmer Winston, chairman of board, dies. Executive vice-president Issac "Ike" Wilson officially takes over duties of chief operating officer.

1940   Deposits at end of year total $89.35 million. Branch in Millington opens. (Between 1940 and 1951, eight more branches go into operation.) *American Banker* ranks Union Planters the nation's 96th largest bank, as measured by deposits.

1941   (June 30): Cleveland Street branch opens at 270 North Cleveland.

1944   Deposits of $193.22 million; resources of $11.40 million.

(June 15): Southside branch opens (84 E. McLemore).

(October): Highland Heights branch opens, 3337 Sumner Avenue.

1946   *American Banker* ranks Union Planters as the largest bank in
        Tennessee and 73rd largest in the nation (based on deposit size).
        Thomas Street branch opens. Name is changed to Union Planters
        National Bank of Memphis.

1947   (July 31): Normal-Buntyn branch opens, 557 Highland Avenue.

1949   (January): 2,218 stockholders; 564 employees. The directors are Vance
        Alexander, Edwin L. Bruce, Robert Carrier, L. B. Lovitt, Joseph
        Maury, Edmund Orgill, Frank Pidgeon, Milton K. Revill, Edward P.
        Russell, and Issac H. Wilson.

        DeSoto branch opens, 124 East Calhoun.

1950   Executive vice-president Ike Wilson dies.

1951   Executive dining room opens.

        (October 10): White Station branch opens, 4900 Poplar.

1952   (April): Arthur McCain elected president; Alexander remains chief
        executive officer and takes the title of chairman of board. Annual
        profit of $1.82 million; 847 employees. Opens expanded and
        redecorated main office.

1953   (July): Interest paid on time deposits goes from 1.5 to 2 percent.

        (November): Union Avenue branch opens.

1954   (October 16): Edward Hull Crump dies.

1955   (January): John E. Brown named president; Arthur McCain is shunted
        into position of vice-chairman of board. Executive vice-president
        Milton Revill dies shortly thereafter. Union Planters is largest bank
        in the Mid-South region of Kentucky, Tennessee, Alabama,
        Mississippi, and Arkansas.

        (December 31): McCain resigns.

1956   (November): Buys three offices of Barretville Bank and Trust
        Company, turning them into branches.

1957   (September): Madison Street branch opens.

1958   (February): Albert M. Brinkley, Jr. joins the bank as intended
        successor to John Brown.

1960   With some 400 country banks as correspondents, Union Planters ranks
        as the 44th largest "banker's bank" in the nation.

1961   Deposits total $406.7 million; annual profit of $4.2 million.

1962   Management steps up the expansion of retail network; between 1962
        and 1968, 13 additional branches go into operation.

1963   (January): Alexander named honorary chairman of board. John Brown officially becomes chief executive officer.

(September): Albert Brinkley, Jr., resigns.

1964   Women are, for the first time, promoted to officers.

1965   27 branches, 1000 employees, 4,000 stockholders.

(July 1): Interest paid on time deposits rises from 3.5 to 4 percent.

North Memphis branch moves into the 100 North Main building.

1966   (January): Board elects C. Bennett Harrison, Jr., president; Brown remains chairman.

(February 15): Vance Alexander dies.

1967   (December 31): Brown resigns and Harrison becomes chief executive.

Union Planters adopts as its trademark a symbol showing three stylized plant leaves within a triangle.

1968   W. Porter Grace named president. Construction begins on a 9-story annex building at the northeast corner of Front and Madison.

1969   Union Planters is 100 years old. Has dropped to 95th place among nation's largest banks, as measured by deposits.

(October): Board moves Grace to vice-chairmanship and elects James C. Merkle president. Work force of 1,322; 31 branch offices.

1971   Deposits top $1 billion.

1972   (July): Organizes a holding company, Union Planters Corporation (UPC).

(August): Acquires Percy Galbreath & Son, a mortgage banking firm.

1973   (September): Management charges off $6.5 million in loans, or 50 percent more than during the previous year. A $1 million loss is discovered in the trading account.

(November 23): James Merkle resigns from the presidency, and Harrison assumes that title.

1974   (January): George C. Webb named president.

(May 13): William M. Matthews, Jr. elected president of UPC.

(August 1): Sells 100 North Main Building.

(October 17): Harrison resigns all offices; Matthews officially becomes chief executive; Richard A. Trippeer, Jr., replaces Webb as president of Union Planters National Bank (UPNB).

(December): Year-end loss of $16.75 million. Management learns of potentially massive losses in commercial lending. Bond claims of more than $16.5 million are filed against surety companies. The bank's first automatic teller machines (ATMs), dubbed "Annie," are in operation.

1975   (July 1): L. Quincy McPherson elected vice-chairman of Union Planters Corporation (UPC).

(December 16): Sixteen criminal indictments returned against former officers. Loan volume has fallen from $744,464 (at end of 1973) to $487,995. During same period deposits fell from $1.03 million to $824,586. Year-end loss of $2.75 million. 1,623 employees.

1976   Operations are re-organized into four groups: *Commercial* (agriculture, national and metro accounts, investment, international, real estate, and marketing) under Quincy McPherson; *Greater Memphis Group* (automation, operations, retail, consumer lending) under Benjamin W. Rawlins, Jr.; *Staff* (personnel, loan administration, and finance) under Rudolph Holmes; and *Trust,* under James F. Springfield.

(December): Annual loss of $834,454.

1977   (June–July): Awarded $10.8 million on bond claims.

(December): Annual profit of $3.34 million.

1979   Management forms the Investment Banking Group and launches several high-tech divisions. Profit for year of $8.77 million. 1,340 employees.

1980   Earnings of $9.82 million for the year.

1981   Acquires Hamilton First Bank of Clinton and Oak Ridge. IBG accounts for 25 percent of profits, which total $9.83 million.

1982   (September): Ben Rawlins and Quincy McPherson resign. Year-end profit of $11.08 million.

1983   Sells main office at 67 Madison Avenue.

(May 27): Buys from FDIC for $125 million The United Southern Bank of Nashville and United American Bank of Chattanooga.

1984   (September): Matthews resigns; Board elects Ben Rawlins chief executive officer. Year-end loss of $18.78 million; dividends suspended until capital-to-asset ratio improves.

1985   (April): J. Armistead Smith is elected president of UPNB.

(December): Profit of $11.2 million; 24 branches in Memphis and 21 elsewhere in Tennessee; 1,750 employees. Operations are organized into three groups: *Banking* (retail and commercial) under J. Armistead Smith; *Financial Services* (trust, IBG, treasurer's division) under Warren Creighton; and *Bank Administration* under David L. Wark.

1986   Office of Comptroller of Currency releases UPC from consent agreement. Management signs letters of intent to acquire by merger four Tennessee banks.

(December): $19.1 million profit; 1,604 employees.

1987   (January): dividends are reinstated.

(May): Acquires Bank of Roane County with deposits of $107 million and six offices in upper East Tennessee.

(June): Acquires Merchants State Bank with $94 million in deposits and five offices in Middle Tennessee; also acquires FirstBanc of Crossville (Tennessee) with $99 million of deposits, and First Citizens Bank of Hohenwald, Tennessee (deposits of $38 million).

Profits of $10.68 million. UPC ranked as fifth largest bank holding company in Tennessee, 200th in the nation (based on deposits). Assets of $2.3 billion; deposits of $1.6 billion.

1988   (May): Acquires Citizens Bank of Crossville.

(November): Acquires Pickett County Bank and Trust Company, headquartered in Byrdstown, Tennessee. Annual profit of $25.6 million.

1989   (February): Acquires United Southern Bank (chartered in 1900 as the Bank of Clarksdale) with 17 offices in a 7-county area of northwest Mississippi.

(May): Acquires Cumberland City Bank, in Stewart County, Tennessee.

(April 1): Richard Trippeer, Jr., retires as chairman of UPC. Board elects Rawlins chairman and chief executive of UPC and UPNB. Smith becomes vice-chairman of UPC, and Jackson W. Moore is elected president of UPC. Additional members of senior management are Robert L. Booth, Jr. president of the urban banking group; James A. Gurley, vice-president of UPC; John W. Parker, executive vice-president of UPC; Kenneth W. Plunk, president of the community banking group; James Springfield, secretary and general counsel of UPC and UPNB; and M. Kirk Walters, treasurer and chief accounting officer.

(November): Acquires First National Bank of New Albany, Mississippi, with ten offices in a four-county area; also acquires the Citizens Bank & Trust Company of Wartburg, Tennessee, and the Steiner Bank, of Birmingham, Alabama.

(December): Year-end loss of $22.3 million.

1990   (June): Acquires North Arkansas Bancshares, headquartered in Jonesboro, Arkansas.

(December): Annual profit of $22.7 million. Union Planters has assets of $4 billion, deposits totalling $3.34 billion, and operates 56 offices in Tennessee as well as offices in Mississippi, Arkansas, and Alabama.

1991   (January): Broker-dealer operations are spun off into a limited partnership formed with Vining-Sparks Securities, Inc.

Main office staff moves from downtown location at 67 Madison to a new, 5-story administrative center in the Memphis suburb of Cordova.

Year-end earnings of $27.5 million.

1992   (March): Acquires Fidelity Bancshares based in Nashville and purchases $585 million in deposits of Metropolitan Federal Savings and Loan, a Nashville thrift with 17 branches.

(November): Acquires Bank of Commerce, Woodbury, Tennessee.

1993   Completes 12 acquisitions: Bank of Tennessee, Morristown; SaveTrust Federal, Dyersburg, Tennessee; Security Trust Savings, Knoxville, Tennessee; First Federal Savings, Maryville, Tennessee; First State Bancshares, Somerville, Tennessee; Farmers Union Bank, Ripley, Tennessee; Garrett Bancshares, Goodlettsville, Tennessee; Erin Bank & Trust, Erin, Tennessee; Hogue Holding Company, Weiner, Arkansas; Central State Bancorp, Lexington, Tennessee; First Financial Services, Brownsville, Tennessee; First Cumberland Bank, Madison, Tennessee; and the Knoxville offices of Bank of East Tennessee.

Kenneth Plunk is elected president of UPB, and Armistead Smith named President of the Community Banking Group.

(June): Acquires Southeastern Bancshares, parent of the DeKalb County Bank in Alexandria, Tennessee.

Executive management consists of Benjamin W. Rawlins, Jr., chairman and chief executive officer; Jackson W. Moore, president UPC; Kenneth W. Plunk, president UPB; J. Armistead Smith, vice-chairman UPC; Jack W. Parker, chief financial officer; James A. Gurley, executive vice-president; M. Kirk Walters, treasurer and chief accounting officer; and James F. Springfield, secretary and general counsel.

(November): The board of UPC announces plans to charter new Union Planters banks in Chattanooga, Jackson, Knoxville, and Nashville.

(December): Annual earnings of $63.1 million. UP has assets of $6.3 million, deposits totalling $5.3 million, and operates a statewide branch system in Tennessee as well as 35 subidiary banks in Alabama, Arkansas, Kentucky, Mississippi, and Tennessee.

1994   (January-March): Completes four acquisitions: Mid-South Bancorp, Franklin, Kentucky; First National Bancorp, Shelbyville, Tennessee; Anderson County Bank, Clinton, Tennessee; and First National Bank, Clinton, Arkansas.

(April): New headquarters building of UPB opens at 6200 Poplar Avenue, Memphis.

(September): Union Planters observes the 125th anniversary of its formation.

Appendix B

Cohn, Harry	1907–c.1927
Colbert, Robert B., Jr.	1968–
Condon, Martin, J., III	1952–1976
Cooper, John A., Jr.	1973–1974
Craig, R. G.	1891–1895
Dillard, John W.	1899–1919
Dobbs, James K., Jr.	1955–1973
Dockery, J. M.	1899–1919
Dozier, Richard M.	1933–1943
Early, W. C.	1907–1917
Egan, A. H.	1924–1933
Ensley, Enoch	1873–1891
Erb, Louis	1890–1900
Estes, Zenos N.	1869–1872
Falls, J. N.	1895–1899
Farrell, Hanford F., Jr.	1984–
Farrington, William M.	1869–1876
Fitzhugh, Guston T.	1907–1929
Fly, J. M.	c.1924–c.1926
Fogelman, Robert F.	1985–1989
Fontaine, Noland	1898–1912
Fontaine, Noland, Jr.	1912–1929
Frank, J. F.	1885–1886
Frayser, R. Dudley	1885–1889
Friedman, Issac	1891–1892
Gage, W. E.	1907–1922
Galbreath, William B.	1869–1886
Galbreath, William D.	1966–1978 and 1985
Gates, W. B.	1902–1919
Gilleas, M.	1899–1908
Goodbar, J. M.	1907–1917
Goodwyn, William A.	⎰ 1871–1873 ⎱ 1892–1898
Goyer, Charles Wesley	1869–1881
Grace, W. Porter	1963–1972
Greenlaw, William Borden	1869–1875
Grosvenor, Charles N.	1890–1898
Halloran, Fred O.	1933–c.1937
Harper, James L.	1992–
Harrison, C. Bennett	1966–1974
Hayden, Frank	1924–1929
Heflin, John J.	1925–1933

Hill, Frank Fontaine	1897–1924
Hill, Frank F., Jr.	1923–1925
Hill, Napoleon	1869–1909
Holmes, J. E.	1924–1933
Holst, J. F.	1907–1922
Hooper, George H.	1924–1929
House, Emmett J.	1953–1967
Howell, Henry B.	1875–1885
Hudson, Charles	c.1924–1926
Humes, L. C.	c.1924–1926
Humphreys, Cecil C.	1964–1984
Hunter, James F.	1907–1915
Jackson, Thomas H.	1914–c.1926
Jarnigan, M. P.	1875–1883
Johnson, John	1869–1872
Johnston, R. O.	1933–c.1936
Jones, R. L.	1907–1916
Jordan, R. Lee	1918–c.1926
Jurden, Ralph L.	c.1924–1929
Keyes, J. W.	1906–1933
Kopald, S. L., Jr.	1962–1983
Latham, Thomas J.	1884–1885
Leatherman, Samuel R.	1913–1922
Lee, Robert Edward	1924–1933
Lovitt, Lloyd B.	1932–1960
Lovitt, Lloyd B., Jr.	1978–1982
Loeb, William L.	1933–1942
Lowrance, C. J., Jr.	1950–1969
Lowrance, C. J. III	1970–
Lyle, Russell M.	1963–1976
McCain, Arthur W.	1952–1955
McCallum, Robert D.	1972–1980 and 1985
McClure, J. W.	1917–c.1926
McCormack, J. M.	1907–1937
McDavitt, J. H.	1884–1901
McDowell, John D.	1917–1924
McKay, A. N.	1876–1886
McKee, Lewis	1963
McKee, W. Lytle	1929–1948
Mallory, B. Lee	1907–1931
Martin, John D.	c.1915–1929
Martin, R. Brad	1985–

Matthews, William M., Jr.	1974–1984
Maury, Joseph E.	1925–1951
Meacham, M. I.	1869–1895
Merkle, James C.	1969–1973
Moore, Jackson W.	1986–
Hirsch, Morris	1929–c.1934
Murff, J. T.	1964–1982
Nichols, Doddridge	1946–1947
Norfleet, Frank M.	1907–1921
Norfleet, Jesse P.	1918–1922
Owen, C. Penn, Jr.	1978–
Orgill, Edmund	1942–1955
Orgill, William	1926–1940
Overton, Stanley D.	1992–
Peacock, Edward P.	1930–1932
Pepper, John R.	1885–1916
Perkins, Newton C.	1914–1915
Pidgeon, Frank	c.1951–c.1958
Pidgeon, James	1961–1964
Pidgeon, Phil	1940–1946
Plunk, Kenneth	1992–
Polk, Robert S.	1917–1924
Potter, Edward, Jr.	1929–1930
Prescott, William J.	1924–1933
Price, Thomas R.	1974–1988
Randolph, Wassell	1929–1933
Rawlings, J. J.	1869–1876
Rawlins, Benjamin W., Jr.	1984–
Rawlins, Dr. V. Lane	1991–
Read, Samuel P.	1869–1915
Read, Theodore	1903–1918
Reichman, John A.	1924–1930
Revill, Milton K.	1950–1955
Rogers, James A.	1869–1871
Russell, Edward P.	1933–1969
Salsbury, Lant K.	1924–1929
Shannon, Jack T.	1967–1984
Smith, J. Armistead	1987–
Snowden, Isaac N.	1884–1891
Spinning, H. S.	1899–1905
Steinberg, S.	1924–1933
Stratton, John T.	1872–1874

Stratton, Leslie M.	1918–1933
Stratton, Leslie M., Jr.	1952–1954
Stratton, Leslie M. III	1956–
Sturdivant, Mike P.	1990–
Taylor, Hillsman	1929–1930
Tefft, Edward C.	1929–1933
Treadwell, Allison C.	1872–1885
Treadwell, George H.	1965–1970
Treadwell, Timmons L. III	1971–1993
Trippeer, Richard A.	1952–1972
Trippeer, Richard A., Jr.	1973–
Tully, John M.	1967–1993
Turner, Cooper	1966–1973
Turner, T. B.	1875–1884
Tutwiler, Thomas H.	c.1926–1938
Vaccaro, Antonio	1869–1900
Walsh, John T.	1916–1928
Warner, Edwin	1929–1930
Webb, George C.	1955–1980
White, Frank H.	1890–1896
White, William	1929–1930
Wilkins, J. S.	1874–1877
Williams, P. P.	1907–1914
Williamson, William A.	1869–1896
Willingham, E. G.	1931–1940
Wilson, Isaac H.	1933–1951
Winkelman, Henry T.	1907–1938
Winston, Gilmer	1915–1939
Winston, Phillip	c.1939–1942
Woolfolk, Ellis T.	1950–1973

Appendix C

William M. Farrington	1869–1874
Charles Wesley Goyer	1874–1881
Allison C. Treadwell	1881–1885
Napoleon Hill	1885–1897
Samuel P. Read	1897–1915
Frank F. Hill	1915–1924
Frank Hayden	1924–1929
William White	1929–1930
Edward P. Peacock	1930–1932
Gilmer Winston	1932–1933
Vance J. Alexander	1933–1963
John E. Brown	1963–1967
C. Bennett Harrison	1967–1974
William M. Matthews, Jr.	1974–1984
Benjamin W. Rawlins, Jr.	1984–

Index

By John Longwith

Building to Last:
The Story of the American National Bank and Trust Company
(1984)

Castle on a Cliff:
A History of Baylor School
(1994)

Provident:
A Centennial History
(1986)

Since Before the Yellow Fever:
A History of Union Planters Bank
(1994)

The Spark of Enterprise:
A History of Dixie Foundry—Magic Chef, Inc.
(1988)

Since Before the Yellow Fever

Designed by Design For Publishing
Jacket Design by David Bankston
Text and Display type is Times
Manufactured by Arcata Graphics, Kingsport, Tennessee